REVISE KEY STAGE 2 SATs
Mathematics

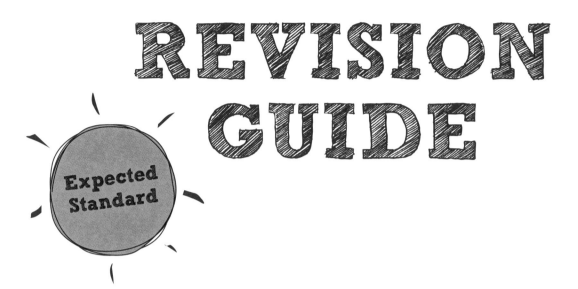

REVISION GUIDE

Expected Standard

Series Consultant: Janice Pimm

Authors: Paul Flack, Hilary Koll and Steve Mills

This revision guide is written for students who aim to perform at the expected national standard in Mathematics in their Year 6 SATs.

For students who hope to perform above the expected standard, check out:

Revise Key Stage 2 SATs Mathematics Revision Guide:
Above Expected Standard   9781292146256

Revise Key Stage 2 SATs Mathematics Revision Workbook:
Above Expected Standard   9781292146270

For the full range of Pearson revision titles visit:
www.pearsonschools.co.uk/revise

WAYS LEARNING

PEARSON

Contents

Number

Calculation

Fractions, decimals and percentages

Ratio and proportion

Algebra

Measurement

Geometry

Statistics

A small bit of small print

The Standards and Testing Agency publishes Sample Test Materials on its website. This is the official content and this book should be used in conjunction with it. The questions in *Now try this* have been written to help you practise every topic in the book. Remember: the real test questions may not look like this.

Introduction

About your tests

At the end of Year 6, you will take tests to find out about your maths skills. This book will help you revise all of the important skills you need for your tests.

- There will be one **arithmetic** test. This test will ask you to carry out calculations. You will have 30 minutes to do this test.

- There will be two **reasoning** tests. These tests will ask you to solve problems. You will have 40 minutes to do each test.

Using this book

Each page of this book is about a different maths skill. Use the checkboxes at the top of the page to track your progress:

Had a look ☐ Tick this box when you've read the page.

Nearly there ☐ Tick this box when you understand the page quite well.

Nailed it! ☐ Tick this box when you understand the page really well.

A note for parents

"Revision is often a problem because a child has become 'stuck'. Either they cannot remember, or they missed something, or they are just confused – but there are one or two bits of maths where they have a problem.

This revision guide is really helpful as each page has an explanation of **how** to do the maths, as well as one or two worked examples. They also show clearly how to lay out the calculations.

It is really confusing for children to be taught a new method at the last moment, so having this shown is very useful.

Remember, revising is hard, and so offering a reward after each session may make the revision go twice as smoothly!"

Ruth Merttens (author of Abacus and Co-Director of the Hamilton Trust)

Place value

You need to be able to read and write numbers up to 10,000,000 (ten million) and know the **value** of each digit.

Reading and writing whole numbers

The value of each digit depends on **where** it is in the number. The digit on the right says how many 1s there are. The next digit to the left says how many 10s there are. The next digits are for 100s, 1,000s, 10,000s, 100,000s and 1,000,000s.

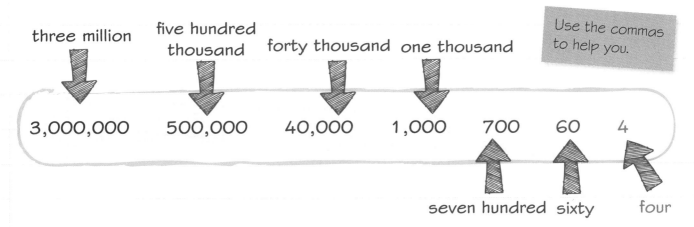

three million   five hundred thousand   forty thousand   one thousand

Use the commas to help you.

3,000,000   500,000   40,000   1,000   700   60   4

seven hundred   sixty   four

3,541,764 ← three million, five hundred and forty-one thousand, seven hundred and sixty-four

Example

Look at this number. 6,345,912
Write the digit that is in the 100s place.   9
Write the digit that is in the 100,000s place. 3

Look at the value of each place in the number.

Now try this

1. What is the value of the <u>underlined</u> digit in each of the examples?
   a) 3,4<u>6</u>5   b) <u>1</u>2,870   c) 9,8<u>7</u>6,490

2. Write the number four hundred and twenty thousand, six hundred and twelve in figures.

3. Write these numbers in words.
   a) 12,850   b) 576,200   c) 8,700,450

Negative numbers

You need to be able to read, write and use **negative numbers** in different situations.

Reading negative numbers

The number line shows positive and negative numbers. Negative numbers are lower than zero. The further away from 0, the lower they are.

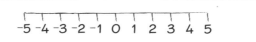

Negative numbers are used to describe temperature. This thermometer shows $-5\,°C$, which is 5 degrees lower than $0\,°C$.

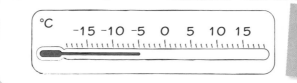

> Here, positive numbers are to the right of 0, negative numbers are to the left of 0.

Using numbers higher and lower than 0

Use a number line to help you add and subtract numbers higher and lower than 0.

To calculate $3 - 7$ start at 3 and move 7 places to the left. $3 - 7 = -4$

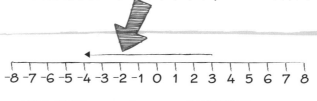

Example

The temperature in London at night was $-3\,°C$. In the day it was 10 degrees warmer. What was the temperature in the day?

$-3 + 10 = 7$

The temperature during the day was $7\,°C$.

> Think of a number line. Start at −3. Count up 10 places.

Now try this

1. Complete the calculation. $6 - 15 =$

2. Find the difference between −7 and 10.

3. At midday the temperature in New York was $3\,°C$. At night the temperature fell by 7 degrees. What was the temperature at night?

Decimal numbers

Each digit to the right of the decimal point is a smaller part of a whole number.

> A longer decimal number is not always worth more. Its value depends on where each digit is.

$$20 \rightarrow 23.468 \rightarrow \begin{array}{l} 0.008 \\ (8 \text{ thousandths}) \end{array}$$

3 — point   0.4 (4 tenths)   0.06 (6 hundredths)

23.468 is smaller than **23.5** (twenty-three point five) because it has fewer tenths.

23.468 is bigger than **23.399** (twenty-three point three nine nine) because it has more tenths.

Example

> More than one of the numbers begins with 56. Compare the values of the digits after the decimal point.

Write the numbers in order from largest to smallest.

| 56.32 | 56.032 | 5.632 |
| 56.199 | 56.302 | |

56.32   56.302   56.199   56.032   5.632

Now try this

1. Write the numbers in order from smallest to largest.

   0.4   4.4   0.14   0.399   0.414   0.44

2. Use the digits 2, 3 and 4 to make four numbers with two decimal places. Write them in order from smallest to largest.

3. Casey has £4.25 pocket money. She spends 20p on sweets and then her mum gives her £1.05

   How much does she have now?

Rounding

You need to be able to **round** numbers.

To round to the nearest 10, look at how many 1s you have.
If you have 5 or more, round up. If you have less than 5, round down.

42 to the nearest 10 is 40 because it is closer to 40 than 50

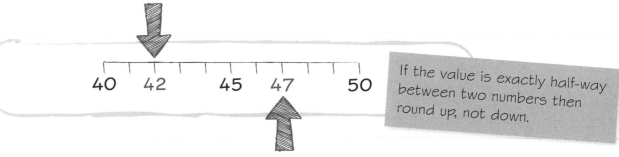

40   42   45   47   50

If the value is exactly half-way between two numbers then round up, not down.

47 to the nearest 10 is 50 because it is closer to 50 than 40

You always follow the same steps for rounding whether you are rounding to 10 or 1,000,000

4,629,712 to the nearest 1,000,000 is 5,000,000

Look at the 100,000s.
4,600,000 is closer to 5,000,000
than 4,000,000 so round up.

Remember to look at the digit to the right of the value you are rounding to. To round to the nearest 100, look at the 10s.

Example

Round 634,585   to the nearest 10,000   630,000
               to the nearest 100   634,600

Now try this

1. Round 5,784 to the nearest 100
2. Round 8,629,299 to the nearest 1,000,000
3. What is 21,247 rounded to the nearest 10?

Rounding decimals

Rounding decimal numbers works in the same way as rounding whole numbers.

3.62 to 1 decimal place is 3.6 because it is closer to 3.6 than 3.7

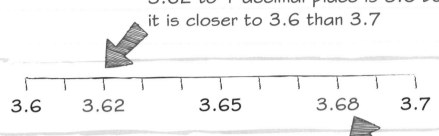

3.6   3.62   3.65   3.68   3.7

If the 2nd digit is 5 or higher, round up. If it is lower than 5, round down.

3.68 to 1 decimal place is 3.7 because it is closer to 3.7 than 3.6

0.724 rounded to 2 decimal places is 0.72 because it is closer to 0.72 than 0.73

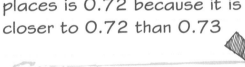

0.72   0.724 0.725   0.728   0.73

0.728 rounded to 2 decimal places is 0.73 because it is closer to 0.73 than 0.72

To round to 1 decimal place, look at the hundredths. To round to 2 decimal places, look at the thousandths.

Example

Round 4.627   to 1 decimal place.   4.6
              to 2 decimal places.   4.63

Now try this

1. Round 6.34 to 1 decimal place.
2. Round 5.569 to 2 decimal places.

Roman numerals

You need to know the **Roman numerals** up to 1,000 and use them to write numbers.

Roman numerals on a clock

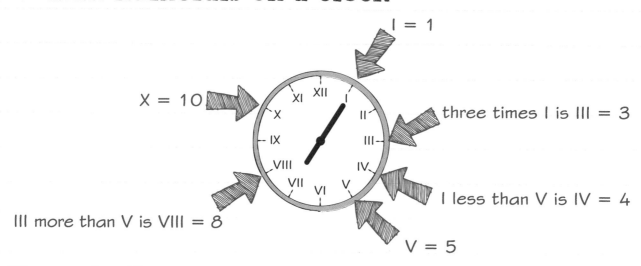

I = 1

X = 10

three times I is III = 3

I less than V is IV = 4

V = 5

III more than V is VIII = 8

Years in Roman numerals

10	20	30	40	50	60	70	80	90	100
X	XX	XXX	XL	L	LX	LXX	LXXX	XC	C

100	200	300	400	500	600	700	800	900	1,000
C	CC	CCC	CD	D	DC	DCC	DCCC	CM	M

Example

What year is MMCXXVII?

M = 1,000 so MM = 2,000   C = 100   X = 10 so XX = 20

V = 5 and II = 2 so VII = 7   Answer = 2127

Now try this

1. What times do these clocks show?
2. Write these years in figures.
   a) MMXX   b) MLXVI   c) MCMLXX

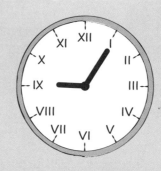
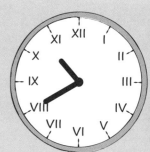

Number and rounding problems

You need to be able to solve number and rounding problems. There might be more than one possible answer to this kind of question.

Number problems

You might be asked to find a number that fits a description.

Example

Find a number between 250 and 299 that is a multiple of 30

Answer = 270

> 300 must be a multiple of 30 so if you subtract 30, the number you get must also be a multiple of 30

Rounding problems

You might be given a rounding fact about a number and asked to find a possible number that it could be.

Example

Kira has two number cards. She writes the numbers to the nearest 10. Both numbers round to 20. She adds the numbers on the cards together and writes the answer to the nearest 10. The rounded answer is 30. What could the numbers be?

> Read the question. It asks you to find two numbers to add together.

If a number rounds to 20, then it must be between 15 and 24. If the total rounds to 30 then it must be between 25 and 34

I need two numbers between 15 and 24 that add together to make a number between 25 and 34

15 + 19 = 34

Answer = 15 and 19

> Try some examples. Does 21 + 15 work? Does 19 + 17 work? There is more than one correct answer.

Now try this

1. Find two numbers with 3 decimal places that add up to 5
2. Elijah rounds a number to the nearest 100. The answer is 200. What is the smallest number it could be?

Written addition

Use columns to do additions that are hard to work out in your head.

Adding using columns

Write the numbers in columns. Line up the 100s, 10s, 1s and so on.

Add the digits in turn. Start with the right-hand column.

If the numbers in a column add to more than 9, move the digits with higher place values to the next column under the answer line.

974.3 + 452.8

```
  974.3        974.3        974.3        974.3        974.3
+ 452.8      + 452.8      + 452.8      + 452.8      + 452.8
  ─────        ─────        ─────        ─────        ─────
      .            .1         7.1         27.1       1427.1
      .           1.          1.         1 1.         1 1.
```

3 + 8 = 11

4 + 2 + 1 = 7

7 + 5 = 12

9 + 4 + 1 = 14

Example

The Adelman family goes on holiday. They drive from London to Paris, then from Paris to Rome, then back to London. How far have they travelled altogether?

	distance (miles)
London to Paris	286
Paris to Rome	1,426
Rome to London	1,878

```
    286
   1426
+  1878
  ─────
   3590
    112
```

Write the numbers in columns. Make sure you line the numbers up.

Now try this

1. What is 3,441 + 6,533?

2. What is 67,739 + 15,426?

3. Estelle scored 45,325 on a computer game and Saskia scored 56,165. What was their total combined score?

Written subtraction

If you can't easily subtract a number in your head, you can use columns to help.

Subtracting using columns

First, write the numbers down in columns with the tenths, 1s, 10s and 100s in line with one another. Make sure that you put decimal points in line too.

Then, subtract from each column in turn, starting with the right-hand column.

There are only 3 in the tenths column.

Move one from the 1s column to make 13 in the tenths column.

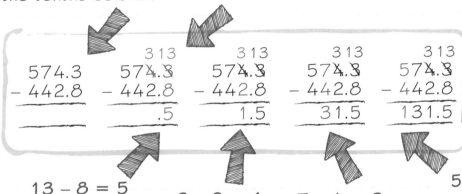

If you don't have enough in one of the columns, you will have to **move** one from the next column.

13 − 8 = 5

3 − 2 = 1   7 − 4 = 3

5 − 4 = 1

Example

Estimate in your head (12,000 − 9,000 = 3,000). Use this later to check your answer.

The Singh family has £12,365 in the bank. They spend £8,700 on a car. How much do they have left in the bank?

```
                        11
               113     0 1 13
  1 2 3 6 5    1 2 3 6 5    1 2 3 6 5
−   8 7 0 0  −   8 7 0 0  −   8 7 0 0
                   6 6 5      3 6 6 5
```

 Cross out any changes and write the new value above.

Answer = £3,665

Now try this

1. What is 3,491 − 2,583?

2. What is £47,739 − £15,826?

3. London to New York is 3,459 miles and London to Tokyo is 5,936 miles. How much further is it to Tokyo from London than to New York?

Estimating

You can use estimates to check an answer to a complicated calculation or work out a rough answer when you don't need an exact one.

Using rounding to estimate

For complicated calculations, use rounding to estimate the answer at the start. If your answer is close to your estimate, you have probably got it right.

> Estimate 3,450 + 3,692 + 9,451 + 750
>
> 3,000 + 4,000 + 9,000 + 1,000 = 17,000

Round to the nearest 1,000

The total of the unrounded numbers is 17,343
This answer is close to your estimate.

Approximating numbers

Use estimates when you do not need an exact number. Sometimes an estimate will tell you all you need to know.

> In February, a football team played three home games. The numbers of fans at the games were 53,629, 48,542 and 45,752. Approximately how many fans went to a home game that month?
>
> 50,000 + 50,000 + 50,000 = 150,000

Round to the nearest 10,000

 **Example**

Round each of the amounts to the nearest pound.

Gael goes shopping. He buys items costing £3.99, £8.99, £4.99 and £1.99. Approximately how much has he spent?

£3.99 ≈ £4   £8.99 ≈ £9   £4.99 ≈ £5   and   £1.99 ≈ £2

£4 + £9 + £5 + £2 = £20

 ≈ means approximately equal to.

Now try this

1. Find the approximate totals.

    a) 6,327 + 3,761 + 7,341 **b)** £3.99 + £6.99 + £9.99 **c)** 0.56 + 2.51 + 4.82

2. At the school fair, Thea sold cakes for £5.99, 75p, £3.30 and £4.75. Approximately how much money did she make?

Add/subtract problems

To solve addition and subtraction problems that are given in words, you will need to decide which calculations to do.

Read, Note information, Calculate, Answer

When solving problems, you can use the letters RNCA (**R**ead, **N**ote information, **C**alculate, **A**nswer) to remind you of some important steps:

Read the question carefully. Ask yourself, 'What am I being asked to find out?'

Note important information (usually numbers).

Identify which calculations you will need to do, choose a method and then **C**alculate. You can use written or mental methods.

Write down your **Answer.** Ask yourself, 'Does it make sense?' and 'Does it answer the question?'

Example

Mari goes ice skating. It costs £4.70. She buys a sandwich and a drink for £2.90. How much change does she have from £10?

£4.70 + £2.90 = £7.60 Add up how much she has spent.

£10 − £7.60 = £2.40 To find out how much money she has left, count up in your head or use a number line.

Mari has £2.40 change. You are asked **how much change** she has. Make sure you complete all the steps.

Now try this

1. Three numbers add together to make 10,000. The first number is 4,625 and the second is 125. What is the other number?

2. Maz has a 5 m length of ribbon. He cuts off two lengths of 1.75 m and one length of 0.35 m. How much ribbon does he have left?

11

Multiples

You need to be able to find multiples of numbers and common multiples of pairs of numbers.

Finding multiples

The **multiples** of a number are all the numbers in its times-table.

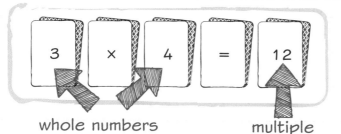

| 3 | × | 4 | = | 12 |

whole numbers   multiple

> 12 is a multiple of 3 and a multiple of 4

Learning your times-tables will help you work out multiples of numbers.

> The first five multiples of 3 are 3, 6, 9, 12 and 15

Finding common multiples

If you compare the multiples of two numbers you will often find that some are the same. These are called **common multiples**.

Multiples of 3
3   6   9   12   15   18   21   24   27   30
Multiples of 6
6   12   18   24   30

Example

> Look for facts you already know. 84 must be a multiple of 7 because 70 + 14 = 84.

Circle all the multiples of 7.

19   ⑭   68   ㊳⁴   32   ⑭⁰   9

Now try this

1. Find all the multiples of 8.   67   64   62   72   76
2. Amelia says that 36,000 is a multiple of 3 and is also a multiple of 6. Is she right? Explain how you know.
3. Bhavnisha is preparing for a party. She has 240 paper cups that she wants to stack in sets of 12. Will all of the sets have exactly 12 cups?

Factors

You need to be able to find factors of numbers and common factors of pairs of numbers.

Finding factors

Factors are the numbers that you multiply together to get multiples.

The factors of 24 are
1 and 24	(1 × 24 = 24)
2 and 12	(2 × 12 = 24)
3 and 8	(3 × 8 = 24)
4 and 6	(4 × 6 = 24)

You can also say a factor is a number that divides exactly into another number.
3 is a factor of 12 because it divides into 12 exactly 4 times.

Finding common factors

If you compare the factors of two numbers you will often find that some are the same. These are called **common factors.**

Factors of 45
1   3   5   9   15   45
Factors of 54
1   2   3   6   9   18   27   54

You will often be asked for the **highest common factor** of two numbers.

Example

Circle all the numbers that are factors of 48

20   (12)   (8)   13   (24)   (16)

Use factors you already know to find ones that you don't.
16 is a factor of 48 because
3 × 10 = 30
and 3 × 6 = 18
so 3 × 16 = 48

Now try this

1. Find all the factors of 64.
34   32   12   36   16   6

2. Look at this calculation.
7 × 3 = 21
Are these statements true or false?

a) 21 is a factor of 7

b) 7 is a multiple of 21

c) 3 and 7 are factors of 21

d) 7 is a factor of 3

Prime numbers

You need to understand what prime numbers are and be able to identify them.

What is a prime number?

You can divide any number by itself and by 1.

$$12 \div 1 = 12$$
$$12 \div 12 = 1$$

Some numbers can **only** be divided by themselves and by 1. These numbers are called **prime numbers**.

> A prime number must have two different factors (itself and 1) so 1 is not a prime number.

The factors of 10 are 1, 2, 5 and 10

The factors of 12 are 1, 2, 3, 4, 6 and 12

The factors of 11 are 1 and 11

The factors of 13 are 1 and 13

10 and 12 are not prime numbers because they have more than two factors.

11 and 13 are prime numbers because they only have two factors.

> Use your times-tables to decide if you can divide each number by a number that is greater than 1. You know that $3 \times 5 = 15$. This means you can divide 15 by 3 and 5 so it cannot be a prime number.

Example

Circle the prime numbers.

15 ⑦ 21 ⑲ 88 ⑤ 20

Now try this

1. Write all the prime numbers between 50 and 60.
2. Alex says, 'If I add together two prime numbers that are greater than 2, I will always get an even number'.
   Is he right? How do you know?
3. Casey says, 'If a number more than 5 ends in a 5, it is not a prime number.'
   Is she right? How do you know?

Square numbers

You need to be able to identify square numbers and you should know how to find them.

Identifying square numbers

A **square number** is a number multiplied by itself.

A square has the same number of dots in each column and each row.

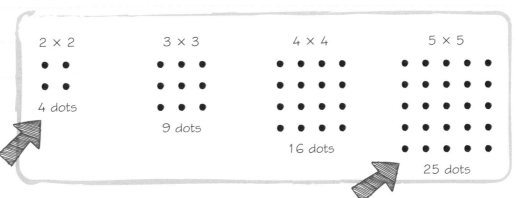

2 × 2
4 dots

3 × 3
9 dots

4 × 4
16 dots

5 × 5
25 dots

25 dots arranged in 5 rows and 5 columns make a square shape so 25 is a square number.

Square powers

You say the number that is multiplied by itself is **squared**.
You write it with a small number 2 to the top right.

8×8 is written as 8^2 45×45 is written as 45^2
$8^2 = 64$ $45^2 = 2,025$

This small number is known as its 'power' so 8^2 could be read as 'eight squared' or 'eight to the power of two'.

Example

Plates of sandwiches at a party are arranged in 9 rows. There are 9 plates on each row. How many plates are there?

$9^2 = 9 \times 9 = 81$

81 plates

The question asks you to multiply 9 by 9. This is the same as 9^2

Now try this

1. Work out the square numbers.

   a) 7^2 b) 8^2 c) 10^2

2. A gardener is putting some plants into pots in a greenhouse. She has 500 rows with 500 pots in each row. How many plants does she have?

Cube numbers

You need to be able to identify cube numbers and you should know how to find them.

Identifying cube numbers

A **cube number** is **three** lots of the same number multiplied together.

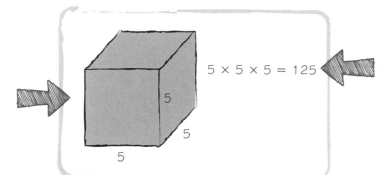

Each side is the same length.

$5 \times 5 \times 5 = 125$

Multiplying the length of a side by itself twice gives you a cube number.

Cube powers

You say the number that is multiplied by itself is **cubed**. You write it with a small number 3 to the top right.

$8 \times 8 \times 8$ is written as 8^3

$8^3 = 512$

$45 \times 45 \times 45$ is written as 45^3

$45^3 = 91,125$

This small number shows how many 'lots' of the number are multiplied together.

Example

Boxes in a shoe shop are arranged in stacks 12 boxes high, 12 boxes across and 12 boxes deep. How many boxes are there?

$12^3 = 12 \times 12 \times 12 = 1,728$

1,728 boxes

Work out $12 \times 12 = 144$ then 144×12. To work out 144×12, you could do 144×10 then 144×2 and add the answers together.

Now try this

1. Work out the cube numbers.

    a) 7^3 b) 9^3 c) 10^3

2. In a coffee shop, cups are stacked neatly behind the counter. They are arranged 4 cups high in rows of 4 and there are 4 rows. How many cups are there?

Short multiplication

You can use short multiplication to multiply by a number with one digit.

Short multiplication

To do short multiplication, write the numbers in columns and multiply each place value in turn.

> Write the numbers you move to different place values under the answer line.

Start with the 1s.
$3 \times 8 = 24$ $2 \times 8 = 16$ $6 \times 8 = 48$

623×8

```
   623          623          623          623          623
×    8        ×   8        ×   8        ×   8        ×   8
_____      _____      _____      _____      _____
                  4           84         4984         4984
   2             12           12           12
```

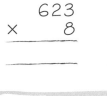
Move the two 10s to the 10s column.

Add on the two 10s to make 18 tens. Move the 1 to the 100s column.

Add on the 1 in the 100s column to make 49 hundreds.

Example

At a restaurant, four friends each order the same meal for £13.75
How much is the total cost?

```
  £13.75        £13.75        £13.75        £13.75        £13.75
×      4      ×      4      ×      4      ×      4      ×      4
_____      _____      _____      _____      _____
               £  . 0        £  .00        £ 5.00       £55.00
                   2          3 2          13 2          13 2
```

Now try this

1. What is 746×7?

2. What is £16.36 $\times$ 9?

3. A ferry travelled from Dover to Calais once a day for a week. There were 1,798 passengers on board during each trip. How many passengers travelled on the ferry in total?

Long multiplication

Long multiplication is like short multiplication except that both numbers can have more than one digit.

Long multiplication

To do long multiplication, separate the smaller number into single digits. Multiply each digit by the larger number then add your answers together.

First write a 0 in the 1s column.

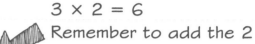
$3 \times 2 = 6$
Remember to add the 2

```
  4 2 7        4 2 7        4 2 7        4 2 7         4 2 7
×   3 6      ×   3 6      ×   3 6      ×   3 6       ×   3 6
      0          ²1 0      1 2 8²1 0    1 2 8²1 0     1 2 8²1 0
                                        2 5¹6⁴2       2 5¹6⁴2
                                                     1 5 3 7 2
                                                       1
```

Multiply each of the digits in the first number by 3. $3 \times 7 = 21$ so write 1 in the 10s column and move 2 to the 100s column.

Now multiply the 1s by each of the digits in the first number.

Add these numbers together.

Example

A sweet shop orders 36 jars of jelly beans. Each jar has 2,648 jelly beans. How many jelly beans are there altogether?

```
  2648          2648          2648           2648
×   36        ×   36        ×   36         ×   36
               7 9⁴4²4 0     7 9⁴4²4 0      7 9⁴4²4 0
                             1 5 8 8 8      1 5 8 8 8
                                           9 5 3 2 8
                                             1 1 1
```

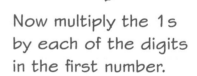

The 3 is three 10s so write a 0. Multiply 2,648 by three 10s. Multiply 2,648 by 6. Then add the answers together.

Answer = 95,328 jelly beans

Now try this

1. What is 4,967 × 64?

2. 9,698 people go to watch a pantomime. They each pay £17 for a ticket. How much money does the theatre collect from the tickets in total?

Short division

You can use short division to divide by a number with one digit.

Short division

Write out the calculation. Write the number you are dividing by on the left.

Divide each digit in turn. 4 won't divide by 6 so include the next digit, which is 2
$42 \div 6 = 7$

$18 \div 6 = 3$

> You could write a 0 in the 1,000s column in the answer to help you keep your numbers in the right columns.

4278 ÷ 6

```
        7           71          713
6)4278    6)4278    6)42⁲7⁸8    6)42⁲7⁸8
```

$7 \div 6 = 1 \ r \ 1$
Move the 1 to the next number to make 18

> If you have a remainder make sure you include it in your answer.

Example

A zoo had 9,576 visitors in 8 days. What was the average number of visitors per day?

```
        1          11         119        1197
8)9576    8)9576    8)9¹576    8)9¹576    8)9¹57⁵6
```

Answer = 1,197

> Be careful to lay out the division correctly.

Now try this

1. Calculate 6,784 ÷ 4.

2. What is £2,590 ÷ 7?

3. Ali has challenged himself to read a book in a week. The book has 364 pages. How many pages does he need to read each day?

Long division

To divide by a number with two or more digits, you can use long division.

$3{,}978 \div 15$

$15, 30, 45, 60, 75, 90$

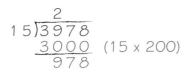

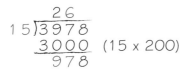

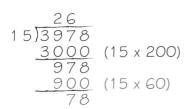

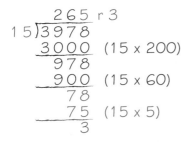

$3{,}978 \div 15 = 265 \text{ r } 3$

Write down the first six multiples of the number you are dividing by.

Look at the first two digits. You can fit 2 lots of 15 into 39 This is the number of 100s. Write 2 in the 100s place.

Work out how much is still left to divide. $15 \times 200 = 3{,}000$ so subtract 3,000

> If the divisor won't fit into the first two digits, look at the first three digits instead.

Look at the first two digits again. You can fit 6 lots of 15 into 97 This is the number of 10s. Write 6 in the 10s place.

$15 \times 60 = 900$ so subtract 900

You can fit 5 lots of 15 into 78 Write 5 in the 1s place.

$15 \times 5 = 75$ so subtract 75 The remainder is 3

> You can also write the remainder as a fraction with the divisor as the denominator.
> $3{,}978 \div 15 = 265\frac{3}{15}$
> $= 265\frac{1}{5}$

Now try this

For simplifying fractions see page 25.

1. Calculate $6{,}928 \div 64$
2. What is £5,061 ÷ 42?
3. 384 pencils are shared equally among 32 children. How many pencils do they each get?

Order of operations

Sometimes a calculation will have more than one part.
You need to know which part to do first.
The rules that tell you which order to follow are called the **order of operations**.

Brackets

Brackets tell us which part of a calculation to do first.

$$4 \times (3 + 7) = 40$$

$$(4 \times 3) + 7 = 19$$

The brackets tell you to do
3 + 7 first.

If the brackets are in a different place,
you might get a different answer.

What to do if there are no brackets

If there are no brackets, follow these rules.

- Do multiplication and division first.
- Do addition and subtraction last.

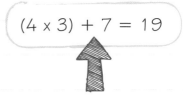

Most people find multiplication and division harder so you can remember this as 'do the harder parts first'!

$$4 \times 3 + 7 = 12 + 7$$
$$= 19$$

Do the multiplication first and then do the addition.

Example

Do the part in the brackets first. Then do the division next, and the addition last.

Calculate $(20 - 4) + 10 \div 2$

$$(20 - 4) + 10 \div 2 = 16 + 10 \div 2$$
$$= 16 + 5$$
$$= 21$$

Now try this

1. Calculate $12 + 6 \div 3$
2. What is $(2 + 8) \times 9 - 2$?

Solving problems

To solve problems with more than one step, you need to decide which calculations to do.

Understanding word problems

To decide how to solve a word problem, remember to **R**ead, **N**ote information, **C**alculate then **A**nswer.

> See page 11 for a reminder of the steps.

> Think about whether it is best to use mental or written methods for each part of the problem.

Example

> To find out how much money they have together, do an addition. To share this amount between the two girls, you need to divide by 2

Maya and Amelia have £30 each. Maya spends £17 and Amelia spends £24. They put their remaining money together and share it equally. How much do they now have each?

Maya has £30 - £17 = £13
Amelia has £30 - £24 = £6
Money put together = £13 + £6
                = £19
Money shared between two = £19 ÷ 2

```
    9 . 5
2)19 .¹0
```

They each get £9.50.

Now try this

1. Two cyclists set off on the same day. The first travels 43 miles a day. The second travels 34 miles a day. How much further ahead is the first cyclist after a week?

2. At the movie kiosk Ellie and Aisha bought some snacks. Aisha bought a drink, some popcorn and a hot dog. Ellie had a drink and some popcorn. Aisha paid £10.95 and Ellie paid £7.20. Popcorn costs £4.65.

   What is the cost of a drink? What is the cost of a hot dog?

Answering the question

Always make sure you answer what the question asks. Read the question before you begin and again after you have found your answer. Does your answer make sense?

Example

If you are working with large numbers, estimate the answer before you begin. When you have worked out the answer, check it against your estimate.

A Year 3 class is going on a trip to the zoo. There are 16 girls, 17 boys, 3 teachers and 5 parents. A mini-bus has 17 passenger seats. How many mini-buses will they need?

Number of people = 16 girls, 17 boys, 3 teachers, 5 parents
Number of seats = 17

 Work out how many people are going by adding together the groups.

16 + 17 + 3 + 5 = 41

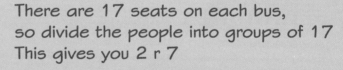 There are 17 seats on each bus, so divide the people into groups of 17 This gives you 2 r 7

41 ÷ 17 = 2 r 7

They will need 3 mini-buses.

 The question asks 'how many mini-buses will they need?' There are 2 full mini-buses and 7 people remaining, so the answer is **3 mini-buses**.

Now try this

Sometimes you only need the whole number and can ignore the remainder.

1. Some children are helping their teacher by sorting coloured pencils into packs of 30. There are 2,570 pencils. How many whole packs will they have?

2. 13 friends are eating pizza at Mabel's birthday party. Each pizza has 8 slices and each person eats 4 slices. How many pizzas did they eat?

Sometimes, you need to write your answer as a fraction to answer the question.

Fractions

You need to understand what a fraction represents.

Fractions as parts of a whole

When you don't have a whole number of something, you can use a **fraction** to describe how much there is. You might have $\frac{1}{2}$ of a chocolate bar or have travelled $\frac{1}{4}$ of the journey.

The bar is divided into seven blocks.

The number above the line is the **numerator** and shows how many parts there are of the whole.

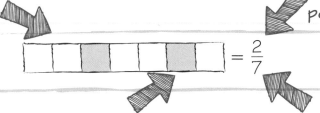 $= \frac{2}{7}$

Notice that it does not matter **which** of the blocks are coloured, the fraction stays the same.

Two out of seven blocks are orange.

The number beneath the line is the **denominator** and shows how many parts make a whole.

Example

What fraction of the diagram has been shaded?

$\frac{5}{10} = \frac{1}{2}$

A useful way to say this is '5 out of 10' as there are 5 blocks coloured orange out of a total of 10

Now try this

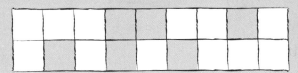

1. What fraction of the diagram is shaded?
2. What fraction of the diagram is unshaded?

Equivalent fractions

You need to be able to change fractions to equivalent fractions. You also need to be able to write a fraction in its simplest form.

$$= \frac{2}{6}$$

$$= \frac{4}{12}$$

The two diagrams both show the fraction $\frac{1}{3}$

Finding equivalent fractions

You can multiply or divide **both** the numerator and denominator by the same number to find an equivalent fraction.

$\frac{1}{3} = \frac{2}{6}$ (multiply both parts by 2) $\frac{4}{12} = \frac{1}{3}$ (divide both parts by 4)

Simplest form

Dividing the numerator and denominator by the same number (a common factor) is called simplifying. If the numerator and denominator do not have any common factors other than 1, the fraction is in its **simplest form**.

For more on factors, see page 13.

$\frac{5}{15} = \frac{1}{3}$ (divide both parts by 5) $\frac{9}{12} = \frac{3}{4}$ (divide both parts by 3)

Example

Susha has 50 counters. 30 are blue and 20 are red.
What fraction of the counters are red?
Write your answer in its simplest form.

$\frac{20}{50} = \frac{2}{5}$

Simplify by dividing the numerator and denominator by 10 to get $\frac{2}{5}$

Now try this

1. Write $\frac{2}{5}$ and $\frac{1}{4}$ as twentieths.

2. Write $\frac{9}{27}$ in its simplest form.

Had a look ☐   Nearly there ☐   Nailed it! ☐

Fractions greater than 1

You need to understand mixed numbers and improper fractions.

Writing mixed numbers and improper fractions

A **mixed number** is made up of a whole number part and a fraction part.

 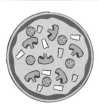  $= 2\frac{4}{5}$ pizzas

There are 2 whole pizzas and $\frac{4}{5}$ of one whole pizza.

In an **improper fraction**, the numerator is greater than the denominator.

   $= \frac{14}{5}$ pizzas

There are 14 slices. Each slice is $\frac{1}{5}$ of one whole pizza.

Converting fractions greater than 1

Example

What is $\frac{20}{3}$ as a mixed number?

$\frac{20}{3} = 6$ whole ones and $\frac{2}{3}$

$= 6\frac{2}{3}$

> To find the number of whole ones, calculate $20 \div 3 = 6$ r 2

Convert $6\frac{3}{4}$ to an improper fraction.

1 whole one $= \frac{4}{4}$ so 6 whole ones $= \frac{24}{4}$

$\frac{24}{4} + \frac{3}{4} = \frac{27}{4}$

> To find the number of quarters in 6 whole ones, calculate $6 \times 4 = 24$ quarters.

Now try this

1. What is $3\frac{1}{2}$ as an improper fraction?   2. Convert $\frac{33}{4}$ to a mixed number.

Comparing fractions

You can compare fractions to decide which one is greater. When you can do this, you can order fractions too.

Fractions with the same denominator

To compare fractions with the same denominator, compare the numerators.

'>' means 'is greater than'.

$\frac{4}{9}$ has more parts of the whole.

$$\frac{4}{9} \quad > \quad \frac{2}{9}$$

numerator
denominator

Fractions with different denominators

To compare fractions with different denominators, look for **common multiples**. This will help you find **equivalent fractions** that all have the same denominators.

For equivalent fractions, see page 25.

To compare mixed numbers, change them to improper fractions. Then the method is exactly the same.

Example

Order these fractions from smallest to largest:

$$\frac{4}{5} \qquad \frac{4}{10} \qquad \frac{1}{4}$$

Change all the fractions to equivalent fractions with 20 as the denominator.

5, 10 and 4 are all multiples of 20

$$\frac{4 \times 4}{5 \times 4} = \frac{16}{20} \qquad \frac{4 \times 2}{10 \times 2} = \frac{8}{20} \qquad \frac{1 \times 5}{4 \times 5} = \frac{5}{20}$$

$$\frac{1}{4} \quad < \quad \frac{4}{10} \quad < \quad \frac{4}{5}$$

Now try this

1. Order these fractions from smallest to largest: $\frac{3}{7}$ $\frac{4}{6}$ $\frac{1}{3}$

2. Ella has completed $\frac{8}{12}$ of her homework. Ben has completed $\frac{7}{9}$ of his.

   Who has completed more of their homework?

Add/subtract fractions

You need to be able to add and subtract mixed numbers and fractions with different denominators. You can use equivalent fractions to help.

Adding and subtracting fractions

Step 1: Convert any mixed numbers to improper fractions.

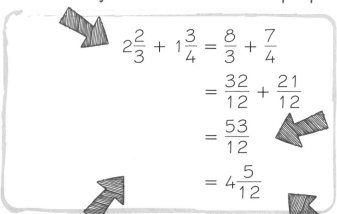

$$2\frac{2}{3} + 1\frac{3}{4} = \frac{8}{3} + \frac{7}{4}$$
$$= \frac{32}{12} + \frac{21}{12}$$
$$= \frac{53}{12}$$
$$= 4\frac{5}{12}$$

Step 3: Add or subtract the numerators.

Step 2: Use common multiples to find equivalent fractions that all have the same denominator.

Step 4: Convert the answer to a mixed number.

Example

Lily painted $\frac{3}{12}$ of a wall, and Daniel painted $\frac{1}{6}$. What fraction has been painted?

$$\frac{3}{12} + \frac{1}{6} = \frac{3}{12} + \frac{2}{12}$$
$$= \frac{5}{12}$$

12 is a common multiple of 6 and 12 so you can find equivalent fractions that both have the denominator 12

Now try this

1. Work out $2\frac{3}{4} + 1\frac{3}{8}$ and write your answer as a mixed number.

2. Work out $5\frac{7}{9} - 2\frac{2}{3}$ and write your answer as a mixed number.

3. In a class, $\frac{5}{8}$ of the children walk to school, $\frac{1}{4}$ cycle, and the rest come by car. What fraction come by car?

Multiplying fractions

You need to be able to multiply simple pairs of proper fractions, and be able to multiply whole numbers by proper fractions.

Multiplying whole numbers by $\frac{1}{2}$, $\frac{1}{3}$ and $\frac{1}{4}$

When you multiply by a proper fraction, the amount becomes smaller.

$$4 \times \frac{1}{4} = \text{four quarters} = 1$$

$$6 \times \frac{1}{2} = \text{six halves} = 3$$

Think about how many 'groups' of that fraction you have. So $4 \times \frac{1}{4}$ is four quarters, which equals 1

Multiplying pairs of proper fractions

To multiply proper fractions, first multiply the numerators, and then multiply the denominators.

Write the calculation horizontally with the numerators and denominators in line.

Multiply across the top and across the bottom.

Write in its simplest form.

$$\frac{3}{4} \times \frac{4}{5} = \frac{3 \times 4}{4 \times 5}$$
$$= \frac{12}{20}$$
$$= \frac{3}{5}$$

Example

One bag of carrots weighs $\frac{1}{2}$ kg. How much will $\frac{1}{4}$ of a bag weigh?

$$\frac{1}{2} \times \frac{1}{4} = \frac{1}{8} \text{ kg}$$

Multiply the numerators and the denominators. Notice that the answer is smaller than either starting fraction.

Now try this

1. What is $\frac{4}{5} \times \frac{1}{8}$?

2. What is $\frac{3}{4} \times \frac{2}{8}$?

3. What is half of $\frac{6}{9}$?

Dividing fractions

You need to be able to divide proper fractions by whole numbers.

Dividing a fraction by a whole number

To divide a proper fraction by a whole number, multiply the denominator of the fraction by the whole number. This gives you the denominator of your answer.

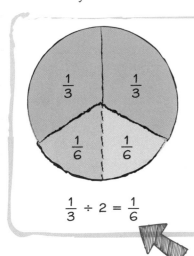

$$\frac{1}{3} \div 2 = \frac{1}{6}$$

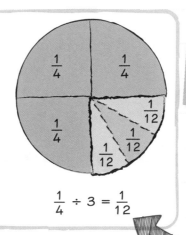

$$\frac{1}{4} \div 3 = \frac{1}{12}$$

If you are dividing a fraction by a whole number, the numerator will always stay the same.

Multiply 3 (the denominator) by 2 (the whole number) to get 6 (the denominator of the result).

Multiply 4 by 3 to get 12 (the denominator of the result).

Example

Oliver shares $\frac{1}{2}$ a pizza equally with two of his friends. How much pizza do they have each?

Half a pizza is shared between 3 people, so $\frac{1}{2}$ is divided by 3

$$\frac{1}{2} \div 3 = \frac{1}{6} \text{ of the pizza each}$$

Now try this

1. What is $\frac{1}{4} \div 2$?

2. What is $\frac{1}{3} \div 5$?

3. Alfie has a bag of 24 sweets. He gives half to his sister Emily, who shares them equally with her friends Alex, Rajesh and Ella. What fraction of the sweets does Ella get?

Equivalent decimals and fractions

You will need to find decimal equivalents for simple fractions.

Fractions out of 10, 100 and 1,000

Fractions with 10, 100 or 1,000 as denominators convert easily to decimals.

> The division sign ÷ is the same as the fraction sign $\frac{\Box}{\Box}$. Both mean something 'out of' something or $\frac{\text{something}}{\text{something}}$.

$$\frac{1}{2} = \frac{5}{10} = 0.5 \qquad \frac{1}{4} = \frac{25}{100} = 0.25 \qquad \frac{3}{4} = \frac{75}{100} = 0.75$$

Using written division

To find the decimal equivalents of other fractions, use written division to divide the numerator of the fraction by its denominator.

Write 5 as 5.000 and divide by 8

Don't forget the decimal point in your answer.

$$\frac{5}{8} = 5 \div 8$$

8	5	.	0	0	0

		0	.	6	2	5
8	5	.	0	^{5}0	^{2}0	^{4}0

So $\frac{5}{8} = 0.625$

Example

What is $\frac{13}{25}$ as a decimal?

$$\frac{13}{25} = \frac{52}{100}$$
$$= 0.52$$

> By multiplying both the numerator and the denominator by 4, we get the equivalent fraction $\frac{52}{100}$

Now try this

1. Write the following fractions as decimals.

   a) $\frac{16}{20}$ b) $\frac{12}{24}$ c) $\frac{3}{8}$

Multiplying decimals

You need to be able to multiply simple decimals by whole numbers.

Multiplying decimals by 10, 100 and 1,000

To multiply a decimal by 10, 100 or 1,000, you can just move the digits left by one, two or three places. To divide by 10, 100 or 1,000, move the digits right.

$$3 \quad \xrightarrow{\div 100} \quad 0.03 \quad \xleftarrow{\times 100}$$

Multiplying decimals by other numbers

You can use multiplying by 10 and 100 to help you with multiplying decimals by other numbers. Follow these steps:

1. Multiply the decimal by 10 or 100 to get a whole number.

2. If the multiplication is too hard to do in your head, use written multiplication.

3. Divide by the same amount as you multiplied by.

See page 17 for written multiplication.

4. Check your answer by doing an estimate in your head.

Example

Calculate 9×1.35

There are two decimal places, so you need to multiply by 100 to get a whole number.

$1.35 \times 100 = 135$
$9 \times 135 = 1,215$
$1,215 \div 100 = 12.15$

Estimate to check your answer. 10×1.35 would be 13.5 so the answer makes sense.

Answer $= 9 \times 1.35 = 12.15$

Now try this

1. Multiply 0.015 by 1,000
2. What is 2.25×7?

Percentages

You need to recognise the % symbol and understand what percentage means.

Understanding percentages

Percentage means per one hundred or **out of 100**

10 green squares out of

$100 = \dfrac{10}{100} = 10\%$

20 red squares out of

$100 = \dfrac{20}{100} = 20\%$

35 yellow squares out of

$100 = \dfrac{35}{100} = 35\%$

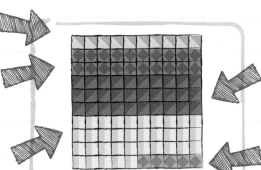

30 blue squares out of

$100 = \dfrac{30}{100} = 30\%$

5 purple squares out of

$100 = \dfrac{5}{100} = 5\%$

Sometimes you will need to write a number as a percentage, but the number of parts that make up the whole will not be 100. You will need to multiply or divide to find your amount **out of 100**

15 out of 50 = 30 out of 100

$\quad = \dfrac{30}{100}$

$\quad = 30\%$

200 = 25 out of 100

$\quad = \dfrac{25}{100}$

$\quad = 25\%$

Example

Rueben has 100 toy cars. 27 of them are blue. What percentage are not blue?

$100 - 27 = 73$

Blue $= \dfrac{27}{100}$ Not blue $= \dfrac{73}{100}$

Not blue $= 73\%$

27 cars out of 100 are blue, so 73 are not blue. There are 100 cars altogether so 73% are not blue.

Now try this

1. James has 50 counters. 25 of them are yellow. What percentage are yellow?

2. 50% of the children in a class walk to school, 25% cycle, and the rest come by car. What percentage of children come by car?

33

Converting percentages

You need to be able to convert percentages to fractions or decimals.

Converting common percentages

Here are some common percentages and their equivalent decimals and fractions.

percentage	fraction	simplified fraction	decimal
10%	$\frac{10}{100}$	$\frac{1}{10}$	0.1
50%	$\frac{50}{100}$	$\frac{1}{2}$	0.5
25%	$\frac{25}{100}$	$\frac{1}{4}$	0.25
75%	$\frac{75}{100}$	$\frac{3}{4}$	0.75
1%	$\frac{1}{100}$	$\frac{1}{100}$	0.01
20%	$\frac{20}{100}$	$\frac{1}{5}$	0.2

Converting percentages to decimals

It is useful to be able to convert between decimals and percentages.

To convert a decimal to a percentage, multiply by 100
To convert a percentage to a decimal, divide by 100

Example

Write 22% as a decimal.

$22 \div 100 = 0.22$

Write 0.33 as a percentage.

$0.33 \times 100 = 33\%$

Now try this

1. Write 65% as a decimal.
2. Write 0.74 as a percentage.
3. Write 15% as a decimal.

Percentages of amounts

You need to know how to find a percentage of an amount.

Finding a familiar percentage

You can find familiar percentages in your head.

Divide by 2   Divide by 4   Divide by 10

| 50% of 4 = 2 | 25% of 32 = 8 | 10% of 200 = 20 |

Finding different percentages

For other percentages you can find a familiar percentage, then multiply or divide your answer to find the percentage you need.

35% of 40

10% of 40 = 4

5% of 40 = 2

35% of 40 = 14

 Find 10% then divide by 2 to find 5%

 Multiply 5% by 7 to find 35%

Example

James scored 80% in a test with 25 questions. How many did he get right?

10% of 25 = 2.5
80% of 25 = 2.5 × 8
          = 20

Now try this

1. What is 25% of 3,200?

2. Find 45% of 350

3. Sam and Rani are sorting out a crate of apples on their market stall.
   There are 400 apples. 12% are red and the rest are green.
   How many apples are green?

Solving percentage problems

You need to know how to solve problems involving percentages.

Comparing percentages of amounts

For a percentage problem, you will need to work out percentages and compare them.

Find 10% by dividing by 10 then multiply by 3 to find 30%:
$60 \div 10 \times 3 = 18$

18 is less than 30

Find 10% by dividing by 10 then multiply by 6 to find 60%:
$50 \div 10 \times 6 = 30$

| 30% of 60 = 18 | < | 60% of 50 = 30 |

Example

Lissie's dad says she can have either 2% of £300 or 80% of £8 for washing his car.
Which should she take to make more money?

Find 2% of £300 by finding 1% (£3) and multiplying by 2 to get £6

1% of £300 = £3
2% of £300 = £6

10% of £8 = £0.80
80% of £8 = £6.40

Find 80% of £8 by finding 10% (80p) and multiplying by 8 to get £6.40

80% of £8 > 2% of £300
She should take 80% of £8

Now try this

1. Which is greater, 20% of 900 or 80% of 250?

2. Alex scored 70% in a test that had 50 questions. James scored 40% in a test that had 100 questions. Who got more correct answers?

3. Casey's jeans should have cost £30 but were reduced by 30%. Amerjeet's jeans should have cost £60 but were reduced by 20%. Who saved more money?

Ratio

You need to understand what ratios are and how to use them.

Understanding ratio

A ratio compares the amounts of two or more things in a group.

There are 4 yellow counters for every 1 red counter, so the ratio of yellow to red is 4 : 1

There is 1 red counter for every 2 yellow counters, so the ratio of red to yellow is 1 : 2

Like fractions, you can simplify ratios or write equivalent ratios by dividing or multiplying all of the numbers in the ratio by the same number.

The ratio of red to yellow counters is 2 : 6

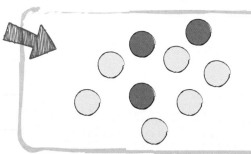

Divide both of the numbers in the ratio by 3 to simplify.
2 : 6 is equivalent to 1 : 3

Multiply or divide both sides of the ratio by the same number to find an equivalent ratio.

Example

To make one pot of pink paint, you mix 1 tube of red paint with 3 tubes of white paint. If you use 12 tubes of white paint, how many tubes of red paint will you need to make pink?

12 ÷ 3 = 4
4 × 1 = 4
4 : 12 is equivalent to 1 : 3
If you use 12 tubes of white paint, you will need 4 tubes of red paint to make pink.

The ratio of red to white paint is 1 : 3 and you have 12 tubes of white paint.
☐ : 12 = 1 : 3

Now try this

1. In a class of 30 children, 18 are girls and 12 are boys. What is the ratio of girls to boys? Remember to simplify your answer.
2. Simplify the ratio 100 : 75

Proportion

Proportion is similar to ratio, but it compares parts with a whole.

Understanding proportion

Proportions are written as fractions because they compare a part with the whole group.

4 counters in total

8 counters in total

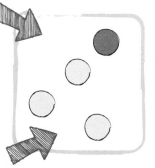

The proportion of red counters is $\frac{1}{4}$ and the proportion of yellow counters is $\frac{3}{4}$

The proportion of red counters is $\frac{2}{8} = \frac{1}{4}$ and the proportion of yellow counters is $\frac{6}{8} = \frac{3}{4}$

Example

How many are there in total? How many parts out of the whole are there?

In a box of books, 5 are fiction and 1 is non-fiction. What proportion of the books is fiction?

6 books altogether
$\frac{1}{6}$ = non-fiction and $\frac{5}{6}$ = fiction

Now try this

1. In a bag of 10 coloured marbles, 7 are yellow and 3 are red. What proportion of the marbles are yellow?

2. In a class survey of 30 children, 15 children said that their favourite colour was blue. What proportion of the class chose a different colour as their favourite?

3. There are 36 skiers in a skiing competition. 6 skiers come from Scandinavian countries. What proportion of the skiers are from Scandinavian countries?

Scale factors

You need to be able to solve problems that involve scale factors.

Similar shapes

You can say two shapes are **similar** if one shape is an enlargement of the other. The **scale factor** tells you how much the shape has been enlarged by.

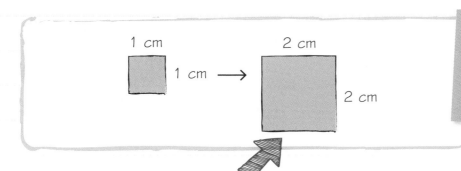

1 cm
1 cm →
2 cm
2 cm

> Scaling can make shapes bigger or smaller.
> The number of sides and the sizes of the angles stay the same.

Each side has been multiplied by 2, so the scale factor is 2

Example

A rectangle measuring 4 cm wide and 7 cm long is enlarged using a scale factor of 3. What are the measurements of the enlarged rectangle?

4 cm x 3 = 12 cm
7 cm x 3 = 21 cm
The enlarged rectangle measures
12 cm wide and 21 cm long.

> A **scale factor of 3** means each side should be multiplied by 3 to get the new length.

Now try this

> If the shape gets smaller, the scale factor will be a fraction.

1. An equilateral triangle has sides of 4 cm. It is enlarged by a scale factor of 5. How long is each side of the enlarged triangle?

2. A regular pentagon with equal sides of 30 cm is scaled so that the sides measure 3 cm. What scale factor was used to scale the shape?

3. A rectangle has sides of 4 cm and 8 cm. After it is enlarged, the shorter side is 10 cm. What is the length of the longer side?

Unequal sharing and grouping

You need to know how to solve problems about sharing and grouping things unequally.

Using ratios for sharing

If you share things unequally, each group gets a different amount. You can use ratios to help you with unequal sharing problems.

> Work out how many parts there are in total and find an equivalent ratio where the two numbers add up to the total number of parts.

Share six sweets between two people so that one person gets twice as many as the other.

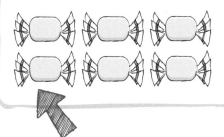
Shared in the ratio of 1 : 2 =

Start with 6 sweets.

For every sweet one person receives, the other person receives 2 sweets.

Example

16 grapes are shared between 2 plates in the ratio of 1 : 3. How many grapes are there on each plate?

There are 1 + 3 = 4 parts in total.
There are 4 lots of 4 parts in 16.
4 × 1 = 4 and 4 × 3 = 12 so the ratio is 4 : 12
One plate has 4 grapes, and the other has 12

> Multiply both sides of the ratio 1 : 3 by 4 (the number of parts that make a whole).

Now try this

1. Sam shares 50 sweets with his sister in the ratio of 2 : 3. He gives his sister the smaller amount. How many sweets does he keep for himself?

2. After 10 weeks, Jack and Thomas have received a total of £40 in pocket money. Thomas gets £3 for every £1 that Jack gets. How much pocket money have they each received?

Ratio problems

You can use your knowledge of multiples to solve ratio problems.

A market stall sells cheese by the kilogram.

1 kg costs £6.70

How much does 500 g cost?

How much does 2 kg cost?

500 g is half of 1 kg
Half of £6.70 = £3.35

For converting units see page 49.

2 kg is twice as much as 1 kg
2 × £6.70 = £13.40

Multiply the price per kilogram by the number of kilograms that you need.

Example

Strawberries cost £3 for 400 g. How much does 1.2 kg of strawberries cost?

1.2 kg = 1,200 g

1,200 g is three times as much as 400 g

£3 × 3 = £9

1.2 kg of strawberries costs £9

Now try this

Multiply both sides of the ratio by the same number to find an equivalent ratio with two numbers that add up to 32.

1. In the supermarket, rice is £2 for 1 kg.
   How much would 5 kg cost?
   How much rice could you buy with £1.50?

2. In a class, the ratio of boys to girls is 3 : 5. If there are 32 children altogether, how many are boys and how many are girls?

Using letters

Sometimes a letter will be used in place of a missing number. You need to be able to work out what the missing number is.

Letters for missing numbers

You can use any letter to represent a missing number.

> I think of a number and subtract four. $a - 4$
>
> I think of a number and multiply by two. $b \times 2$ or $2b$

If you are told the final answer you can write a number sentence.

> I think of a number and divide by three.
> The answer is five. $d \div 3 = 5$ or $\dfrac{d}{3} = 5$

Solving number problems

You can use inverse operations to help you solve number problems like these.

The inverse of an operation is the opposite operation.

operation	+	−	×	÷
inverse	−	+	÷	×

Example

I think of a number and subtract 4.
The answer is 12. What number did I think of?

$a - 4 = 12$
$\quad a = 12 + 4$
$\quad a = 16$

To find a, use the inverse of subtraction which is addition.

Always check by putting your answer back into the number sentence to see if it is correct.
$16 - 4 = 12$ ✓

Now try this

1. Jo thinks of a number, n, and adds 7. The answer is 20.
   Write this as a number sentence. What number was Jo thinking of?

2. a) If $b + 5 = 11$, what number is b?

   b) If $m \times 3 = 15$, what number is m?

   c) If $p \div 2 = 10$, what number is p?

Simple formulae

A formula is a rule for finding an amount. It can be written in words or using figures and letters. You may have to use a formula to solve problems.

Using formulae to solve problems

Formulae is the plural of formula.

A florist uses a formula to work out how much to charge for each bouquet. She charges 20p for each flower plus 50p for the wrapping. She writes *n* for the number of flowers.

Cost = *n* × 20p + 50p

  ⬅ Add 50p for the wrapping.

n is the number of flowers.

Each flower costs 20p.

To work out the cost, replace the *n* with the number of flowers.

For **10** flowers:

cost = **10** × 20p + 50p
　　 = 200p + 50p
　　 = 250p
　　 = £2.50

For **32** flowers:

cost = **32** × 20p + 50p
　　 = 640p + 50p
　　 = 690p
　　 = £6.90

Example

An online bookshop sells books for £3 each plus a delivery charge of £2.50 per order. They write *n* for the number of books. What is the cost for an order of 7 books?

Cost = *n* × £3 + £2.50

Cost = 7 × £3 + £2.50
　　 = £21 + £2.50
　　 = £23.50

Now try this

1. The online bookshop gets an order for 12 books. What is the cost?

2. The bookshop's website says '£5 off your order when you buy 20 or more books'. If a customer orders 25 books, what is the cost?

Linear sequences

When the numbers in a list change by an equal step each time, it is called a **linear sequence**. You need to be able to find missing numbers in linear sequences and write rules to describe them.

Missing numbers

To find missing numbers in a linear sequence, first work out the difference between pairs of number that are next to each other. You can then continue the sequence by adding or subtracting in the same way.

Add 3 to each term to get to the next one.

7, 10, 13, 16, 19, 22, 25 28 31
+ 3 + 3 + 3 + 3 + 3 + 3 + 3 + 3

Subtract 7 from each term to get to the next one.

64, 57, 50, 43, 36, 29, 22 15 8
 − 7 − 7 − 7 − 7 − 7 − 7 − 7 − 7

Term-to-term rule

A **term-to-term rule** tells you the first number in the sequence and describes what you do to each term to get to the next number. You can use a term-to-term rule to generate a sequence.

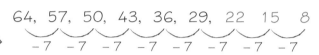

7,   10,   13,   16,   19,   22,   25,   28,   31
64,   57,   50,   43,   36,   29,   22   15   8

The term-to-term rule is **first term = 7, add 3 to each term.**

The term-to-term rule is **first term = 64, subtract 7 from each term.**

Example

Write the first eight terms of this sequence.
First term = 9, add 6 to each term.

Add 6 to the first term to get 15

9, 15, 21, 27, 33, 39, 45, 51

Now try this

1. Write the next three numbers in this sequence. What is the term-to-term rule?
   50, 47, 44, 41, 38, 35, 32...

2. Write the first eight terms of this sequence.
   First term = 17, subtract 3 from each term.

Two unknowns

Number sentences can have more than one unknown number. You need to know how to work out what these numbers could be.

Pairs of solutions

This number sentence has two unknown numbers, shown by the letters a and b.

If $a = 7$, $b = 11$, because $7 + 4 = 11$

If $a = 1$, $b = 5$, because $1 + 4 = 5$

$a + 4 = b$

If $a = -5$, $b = -1$, because $-5 + 4 = -1$

Sometimes you will be told more information about the unknown numbers, which will reduce the number of possibilities. You may be told that a and b are both positive integers less than 8. Then a could only be 1, 2 or 3, and b could only be 5, 6 or 7.

Example

In this equation, n and m stand for positive integers less than 6.

$n - 2 = m$

List all the possible numbers they could be.

When $n = 5$, $m = 3$
When $n = 4$, $m = 2$
When $n = 3$, $m = 1$

> There are no more solutions because if n was 2, $m = 0$ which is not a positive integer.

Now try this

1. Which of these are true for this number sentence? $m + 2 = n$
   a) m could be 4 and n could be 2
   b) m could be 5 and n could be 7
   c) m could be 2 and n could be 4

2. In this equation, n and m stand for positive integers less than 7.
   List all the possible numbers they could be.
   $n - 1 = m$

3. In this equation, a and b stand for positive integers less than 7.
   List all the possible numbers they could be.
   $a + 4 = b$

Combination problems

Combination problems ask you to work through all of the possibilities in a situation.

A T-shirt comes in 3 colours: red, green and blue, and in 3 sizes: large, medium and small. This picture shows all of the different possible T-shirts.

red large · green large · blue large · red medium · green medium · blue medium · red small · green small · blue small

Using a table

You can use a table to show all of the possibilities.

> Write down all of the colour options in each column, and all of the size options on each row.

This column shows all of the colour options for a medium T-shirt.

red	large	red	medium	red	small
green	large	green	medium	green	small
blue	large	blue	medium	blue	small

This row shows all of the size options for a blue T-shirt.

Example

Gareth makes a sandwich from one type of bread with one filling. He can choose white or brown bread, and the fillings are jam, cheese, egg and tuna.

Draw a table of all of the different combinations he could choose.

white	cheese	white	jam	white	egg	white	tuna
brown	cheese	brown	jam	brown	egg	brown	tuna

Now try this

1. A shop sells 4 flavours of smoothie: strawberry, kiwi, banana or mango. You can choose either milk or ice cream to make your smoothie. Draw a table of all of the different combinations of smoothies you can choose.

Algebra problems

You can use algebra to help you solve problems about unknown numbers.

Solving problems with algebra

When trying to solve problems about unknown numbers, it can help to write number sentences and think about the possible numbers that would make them true.

Look at the problem below.

> a and b each stand for a whole number.
>
> a plus b equals 8.
>
> b is three times as large as a.
>
> What are the values of a and b?

Write number sentences to explain the problem.

$$a + b = 8 \quad \text{and} \quad a \times 3 = b$$

Find numbers that fit into one of your number sentences.

$a + b = 8$
If $a = 1$, $b = 7$
If $a = 2$, $b = 6$
If $a = 3$, $b = 5$
If $a = 4$, $b = 4$
If $a = 5$, $b = 3$
If $a = 6$, $b = 2$
If $a = 7$, $b = 1$

Then see which pair of numbers also fits the other number sentence.

$a \times 3 = b$
If $a = 2$, $b = 6$

> Use the information in the question to write number sentences. Then work through all of the possible numbers in order.

Now try this

1. a and b each stand for a whole number. a plus b equals 25
a is four times as large as b. What are the values of a and b?

Reading scales

There are lots of different types of measuring equipment. You need to be able to read the scales to take a measurement.

Find the size of each interval

To read scales, you first find out what each interval is worth.

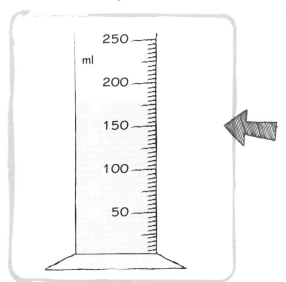

Make sure you count the gaps and not the lines!

There are 10 intervals between 150 ml and 200 ml so each interval is worth 50 ml ÷ 10 = 5 ml.

The liquid comes up to 6 intervals past 150 ml.

Calculate 150 + 6 × 5 = 180 ml

Example

What mass is the arrow pointing to?

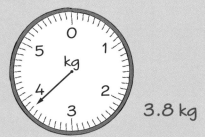

3.8 kg

4 kg − 3 kg = 1 kg.
There are 10 intervals.
Each interval is worth 1 kg ÷ 10 = 0.1 kg.
The arrow is 8 intervals past 3 kg.
The arrow points to 3.8 kg.

Now try this

1. Read each scale.

a)

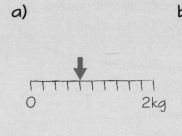

b)

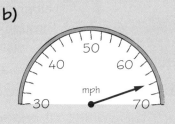

c)

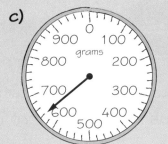

d)

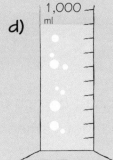

Converting units

You need to be able to convert between units of length, weight and capacity.

Converting between units

Use the table below to help you convert from one unit of length to another.

> Work out how many of the smaller unit there are in the larger unit and multiply or divide by this number.

cm → mm	× 10	m → cm	× 100	km → m	× 1,000
mm → cm	÷ 10	cm → m	÷ 100	m → km	÷ 1,000
kg → g	× 1,000	t → kg	× 1,000	l → ml	× 1,000
g → kg	÷ 1,000	kg → t	÷ 1,000	ml → l	÷ 1,000

Example

Convert these measurements to the units asked for.
1. What is 1.3 cm in mm?
2. What is 2,750 cm in m?
3. What is 3,180 ml in litres?

> cm → mm   × 10
> cm → m   ÷ 100
> ml → l   ÷ 1,000

$1.3 \times 10 = 13$ mm $2,750 \div 100 = 27.5$ m $3,180 \div 1,000 = 3.18$ litres

Now try this

1. a) What is 58 mm in cm?
   b) What is 1.5 m in cm?
   c) What is 7,040 g in kg?
2. Clare weighs some potatoes. The scale shows 4.25 kg. What is this in grams?
3. A jug holds 4.275 l of milk. Zhen pours 700 ml into a saucepan. How much milk is still in the jug?

49

Ordering measures

You need to know the metric units of length, weight and capacity so that you can compare and order measurements.

Types of measurement

There are standard units of measurement for all of the different things that can be measured.

> When comparing measurements, look carefully at the units.

	length	weight	capacity
units of measurement	millimetres, centimetres, metres, kilometres	grams, kilograms, tonnes	millilitres, litres
abbreviation	mm, cm, m, km	g, kg, t	ml, l
examples of measuring equipment	ruler, tape measure, metre stick, trundle wheel	balance scales, kitchen scales, bathroom scales	measuring spoons, measuring jugs

Example

> Convert all of the lengths to centimetres then order the original amounts.

Put these lengths in order of size, starting with the smallest.

2 m   140 mm $\frac{1}{4}$ m   37 cm $\frac{1}{2}$ km   6 cm

2 m = 200 cm   140 mm = 14 cm $\frac{1}{4}$ m = 25 cm

$\frac{1}{2}$ km = 500 m = 50,000 cm

Order: 6 cm   140 mm $\frac{1}{4}$ m   37 cm   2 m $\frac{1}{2}$ km

Now try this

1. Put these capacities in order of size, starting with the smallest.

   820 ml $\frac{1}{2}$ l   742 ml $\frac{3}{4}$ l   482 ml $\frac{4}{5}$ l

2. Put these weights in order of size, starting with the smallest.

   3 kg $\frac{3}{4}$ kg   200 g $\frac{1}{4}$ kg   2,500 g   2 kg

50

Imperial units

You need to know about imperial units and be able to roughly convert between imperial and metric units.

measurement	imperial to metric
length	1 mile ≈ 1.6 km
	1 inch ≈ 2.5 cm
weight	1 pound ≈ 400 g 1 ounce ≈ 30 grams 2.2 pounds ≈ 1 kg
capacity	1 pint ≈ 500 ml

≈ means approximately equal to. Imperial and metric equivalents are not exact so use the ≈ sign to show this.

Miles and kilometres

You need to remember how to convert between miles and kilometres.

To convert from:

miles → km　　**× 1.6**　　　　km → miles　　**÷ 1.6**

A mile is longer than a kilometre so the number of miles will always be **less** than the equivalent number of kilometres.

Example

Approximately how many kilometres are there in 40 miles?
Approximately how many miles are there in 160 km?

40 miles ≈ 40 × 1.6 km
　　　　≈ 64 km

160 km ≈ 160 ÷ 1.6 miles
　　　　≈ 100 miles

Now try this

Use the table at the top of the page to help you.

1. a) Approximately how many kilometres are there in 200 miles?
   b) Approximately how many miles are there in 40 km?
2. Approximately how many millilitres are there in 2.5 pints?

Measure calculations

You need to be able to calculate with measurements that include decimal numbers or different units.

Choosing units

If a question has a mix of different units, choose the units that make the calculation easiest.

If you find it easier to calculate with whole numbers rather than decimals, choose a smaller unit so you don't have to work with decimals.

> Find the sum of 15.7 kg and 5,750 g.
> Give your answer in kilograms.
>
> 15.7 kg = 15,700 g
> 15,700 g + 5,750 g = 21,450 g
> 21,450 kg = 21.45 kg

You could write both measurements as grams or kilograms.

Always give your answer in the units that the question asks for.

Example

Petra posts four parcels, each weighing 0.27 kg.

What is the total weight of the four parcels in kilograms?

Change 0.27 kg to grams. Remember to give your answer in the correct units.

0.27 kg = 270 g

270 × 4 = 1,080 g
        = 1.08 kg

Now try this

1. Find the sum of 2.546 litres and 136 millilitres. Give your answer in litres.

2. Kate's stride is 1.2 m. What is the length of 7 of her strides in metres?

3. Pete went on a cycling holiday. He rode 32 km on the first day, and 46.9 km on the second. He wants to cover 100 km in three days. How far does he need to ride on the third day?

Time

Make sure you are confident in converting between units of time and can tell the time on both digital and analogue clocks.

12-hour and 24-hour time

Clocks can show 12-hour or 24-hour time.

> For 12-hour times, you need to say am (morning) or pm (afternoon).

To go from 12-hour time to 24-hour time, **add** 12 hours to afternoon times only.

analogue 12-hour time

digital 24-hour time

05:15

17:15

To go from 24-hour time to 12-hour time, **subtract** 12 hours from afternoon times only.

Units of time

You should know these relationships between units of time.

60 seconds = 1 minute	7 days = 1 week	12 months = 1 year
60 minutes = 1 hour	365 (or 366) days = 1 year	10 years = 1 decade
24 hours = 1 day	52 weeks = 1 year	100 years = 1 century

Example

The church clock is running 11 minutes fast this afternoon.
What is the correct time? Give your answer in 24-hour digital form.

11 minutes earlier than 5 minutes past 3 is 6 minutes to 3.

2:54 in the afternoon
Answer = 14:54

Now try this

1. How is quarter to seven in the evening shown in 24-hour digital form?
2. The clock on a phone screen shows 19:21. What time will it show 49 minutes later?

53

Perimeter and area

The **perimeter** of a shape is the distance all the way around its edge.
The **area** is the amount of space inside the shape.

Rectangles

To find the perimeter of a rectangle or square, add together
the length (*l*) and width (*w*), and then multiply by 2.

> Perimeter is measured in units of length such as mm, cm or m.

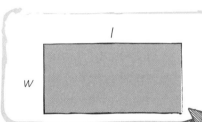

Perimeter of rectangle $= 2 \times (l + w)$

Area of rectangle $= l \times w$

> Area is measured in square units such as mm², cm² or m².

To find the area of a rectangle or square, multiply the length by the width.

Example

Find the perimeter and area of the shapes below.

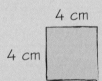

4 cm
4 cm

8 cm
2 cm

> Shapes with the same area can have different perimeters.

Area of square $= 4 \times 4$
$= 16 \text{ cm}^2$

Area of rectangle $= 8 \times 2$
$= 16 \text{ cm}^2$

Perimeter of square $= 2 \times (4 + 4)$
$= 16 \text{ cm}$

Perimeter of rectangle $= 2 \times (8 + 2)$
$= 20 \text{ cm}$

Now try this

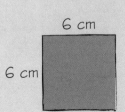

A

6 cm
6 cm

B

12 cm
3 cm

C

5 cm
4 cm

D

10 cm
2 cm

1. Which quadrilateral has the same perimeter as quadrilateral A?

2. Which quadrilateral has the same area as quadrilateral A?

Compound shapes

Compound shapes are made up of other shapes. It is useful to be able to find unknown lengths and to use them to find the perimeters of these shapes.

Finding unknown lengths

You can use the lengths of the sides you do know to work out any unknown lengths.

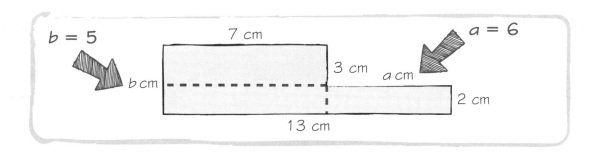

Finding perimeter

First, find the lengths of all of the sides of the shape. Then you can add them all together to find the perimeter.

Example

Find the perimeter of this compound shape.

> Find the unknown lengths first, then add all of the sides together to find the perimeter.

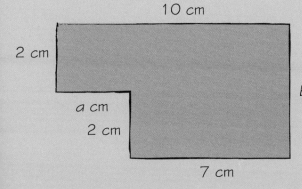

$a + 7 = 10$ so $a = 3$ cm
$b = 2 + 2 = 4$ cm

Perimeter $= 10 + 4 + 7 + 2 + 3 + 2$
$= 28$ cm

Now try this

1. Find the perimeter of the compound shape.

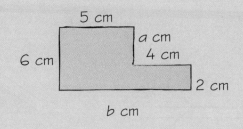

55

Areas of triangles

You need to be able to work out the areas of triangles.

If you cut a rectangle diagonally in half, you get two equal triangles.
The area of each triangle is half the area of the rectangle.

This is the **perpendicular height**.

6 cm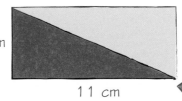

This is the **base** of the triangle.

11 cm

Area of triangle $= \frac{1}{2}$ (base × perpendicular height) or $\frac{1}{2}(b \times h)$

$= \frac{1}{2}(6 \times 11)$

$= 33 \text{ cm}^2$

This formula works for all types of triangles, not just right-angled triangles.

Example

Work out the area of the triangle.

The lengths you multiply together must be at right angles to each other.

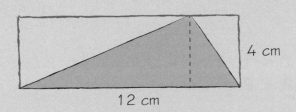

12 cm

4 cm

Area $= \frac{1}{2}(12 \times 4)$

$= \frac{1}{2} \times 48$

$= 24 \text{ cm}^2$

Now try this

1. Find the area of each triangle.

a)

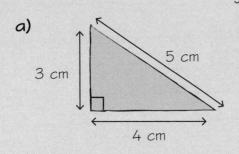

3 cm

5 cm

4 cm

b)

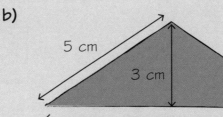

5 cm

3 cm

8 cm

Areas of parallelograms

You need to know how to find the area of a parallelogram.

Moving a triangle from one side of the parallelogram to the other makes a rectangle. The area of the parallelogram is the same as the area of the rectangle.

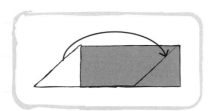

> For more about parallelograms, see page 60.

To find the area of a parallelogram, you multiply the length of the **base** by the **perpendicular height** (the height at right angles to the base).

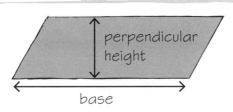

perpendicular height

base

> The lengths you multiply must be at right angles to each other.

Area of parallelogram = base × perpendicular height   or $b \times h$

Example

Find the area of this parallelogram.

> The perpendicular height (at right angles to the base) is 6 cm.

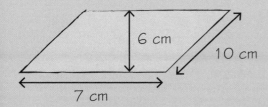

6 cm

10 cm

7 cm

Area = base × perpendicular height
    = 7 cm × 6 cm
    = 42 cm²

Now try this

1. Find the area and perimeter of each parallelogram.

a)

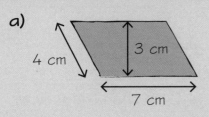

4 cm   3 cm

7 cm

b)

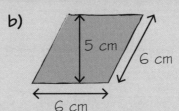

5 cm   6 cm

6 cm

Volumes of cuboids

The **volume** of a 3D shape is the amount of space it takes up. It is measured in cubic units such as cm^3 or m^3. Make sure you can find the volumes of cuboids.

Cuboids

To find the volume of a cuboid, multiply the length (*l*) by the width (*w*) by the height (*h*).

> Make sure you give the correct units in your answers.

Volume of a cuboid = $l \times w \times h$

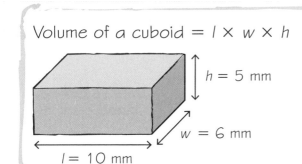

$h = 5$ mm
$w = 6$ mm
$l = 10$ mm

Volume = 10 mm × 6 mm × 5 mm
= 300 mm³

Cubes

The length, width and height of a cube are all the same, so the formula for the volume of a cube can be written as:

Volume of a cube = length x length x length
= $l \times l \times l$
= l^3

Example

A cuboid has a length of 3 m, a width of 2 m and a height of 2 m. What is the volume of this cuboid?

Volume of cuboid = $l \times w \times h$
= 3 m × 2 m × 2 m
= 12 m³

Now try this

1. A cuboid has a length of 4 cm, a width of 3 cm and a height of 2 cm. What is its volume?

2. How much larger is the volume of a cube with sides of 2 cm than the volume of a cube with sides of 1 cm?

2D shape properties

You need to be able to identify the properties of 2D shapes.

Parallel and perpendicular

Parallel lines are the same distance apart from each other along their entire length.

Perpendicular lines are at right angles to each other.

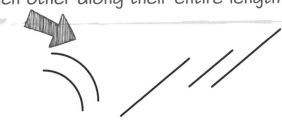 

Regular and irregular shapes

Four equal sides but **not** four equal angles so this quadrilateral is irregular.

> If all the sides of a shape are equal and all the angles are equal, the shape is **regular**.
> Otherwise, it is **irregular**.

irregular

regular

Five equal sides **and** five equal angles so this pentagon is regular.

Example

Here are two sides of a quadrilateral. Complete the quadrilateral so that it has one pair of parallel sides and one right angle. Then name the shape.

A trapezium

> A quadrilateral with one pair of parallel sides is a trapezium.

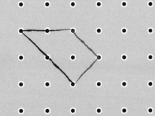

Now try this

For naming 2D shapes see page 60.

1. Name these shapes and say whether they are regular or irregular.

a)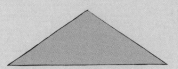

b)

c)

d)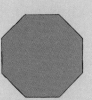

Naming 2D shapes

You need to be able to recognise, name and describe different 2D shapes.

If a shape has only straight sides, it is called a **polygon.**

circle	semi-circle	triangle	quadrilateral	pentagon	hexagon	heptagon	octagon
●	◖	◭	▱	⬠	⬡	⬡	⯃
1 side	2 sides	3 sides	4 sides	5 sides	6 sides	7 sides	8 sides

Different types of triangles and quadrilaterals have special names.

isosceles triangle	equilateral triangle	scalene triangle
2 equal sides 2 equal angles	3 equal sides 3 equal angles	0 equal sides 0 equal angles

rectangle	square	trapezium
2 pairs of equal sides 4 right angles	4 equal sides 4 right angles	1 pair of parallel sides
parallelogram	**rhombus**	**kite**
2 pairs of parallel sides equal opposite angles	4 equal sides equal opposite angles	2 pairs of equal sides 1 pair of equal opposite angles

Neow try this

1. Name these shapes.

a)   b)   c)   d)

Naming 3D shapes

You need to know the names of 3D shapes and be able to recognise them.

Pyramids have a 2D shape for a base, and the rest of the faces are triangles.

Prisms are the same shape along their whole length.

curved 3D shapes			pyramids			prisms		
sphere	hemisphere or cone	cylinder	tetrahedron	square-based pyramid	pentagonal-based pyramid	triangular prism	cube or cuboid	pentagonal prism

Faces, vertices and edges

Count the vertices (corners).

Count the faces and describe their shape.

Count the edges (where faces meet).

Example

Look at this shape. Give:
• its name
• the number and shape of its faces
• the number of vertices and edges it has.

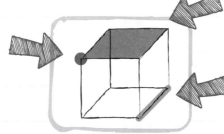

It can help to tick off each corner when counting the vertices.

It is a triangular prism with 2 triangular faces, 3 rectangular faces, 6 vertices and 9 edges.

Now try this

1. Name each shape and say how many faces, vertices and edges it has.

a)

b)

c)

d)

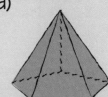

Nets

The **net** of a 3D shape is the flat shape that folds to make the 3D shape. Visualise what the 3D shape will look like, based on the shapes of the faces and how they fit together.

> Imagine folding along each line in the shape to work out how they fit together.

 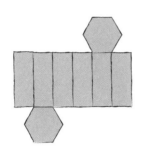  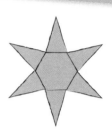

Example

All of the nets below fold to make the same shape. True or false?

> There are actually 11 different nets that fold to make a cube.

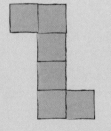 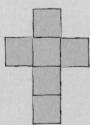 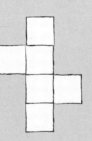 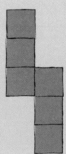 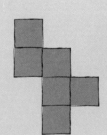 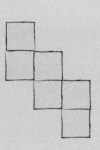

True

Now try this

1. Name the 3D shape that each net folds to make.

a)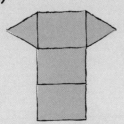

b)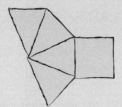

c)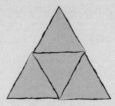

Angles

Using a protractor

Line up the corner of the angle with the centre of the protractor.
Make sure one line of the angle lies along the zero line of the protractor.
Then count around from the zero line.

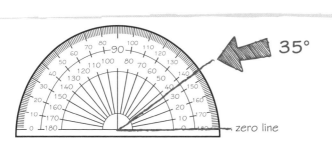 35°

zero line

> Be sure to choose the right scale. Start from zero and follow the numbers around until you reach the line.

Naming angles

right angle (90°)   straight angle (180°)   full turn (360°)

acute angle   obtuse angle   reflex angle
(less than 90°)   (more than 90°   (more than 180°)
                     but less than 180°)

Example

> Line up the bottom of the angle with the zero line and count around from zero.

Measure this angle with a protractor. Say whether the angle is acute, obtuse or reflex.

132° so it is obtuse.

Now try this

1. Use a protractor to measure the angle, and say whether it is acute, obtuse or reflex.

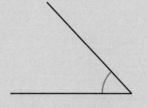

Calculating angles

To find the size of angles without using a protractor, you will need to know these rules.

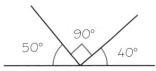

The sum of the angles along a straight line is 180°

The sum of the angles in any triangle is 180°

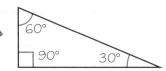

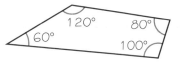

The sum of the angles in any quadrilateral is 360°

The sum of the angles about a point is 360°

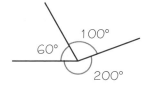

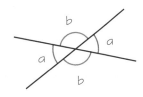

When two straight lines cross, the opposite pairs of angles are equal.

Example

Find the size of the missing angle a.

180° – 20° – 90° = 70°

a = 70°

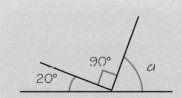

Now try this

You can use the rule about the sum of angles in a triangle.

1. Find the size of the missing angle a in this triangle.

Drawing 2D shapes

To draw 2D shapes, you need to be able to use a ruler and a protractor.

Using a ruler

Make sure the end of the line lines up with the start of the scale (at zero), not with the end of the ruler!

0 1 2 3 4 5 6 7 8 9 10 ✓

Drawing an angle

Draw a line with a ruler first, unless one has been drawn for you.

110°

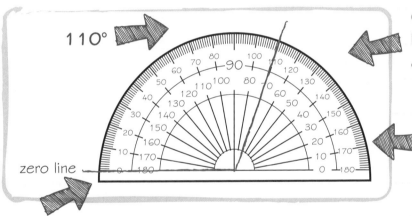

zero line

Count around from the zero line to the angle you are drawing and make a mark.

Join the end of the line to the mark. Use a ruler.

Make sure the zero line of the protractor lies along the line.

Remember to use the correct scale on the protractor.

Now try this

Use a ruler and a protractor for these questions.
1. Make an accurate drawing of a right-angled triangle with a 7 cm base and one angle of 35°.
2. Make an accurate drawing of an isosceles triangle with an 8 cm base and two angles of 73°.

Circles

Make sure you learn the names of the features of circles and can recognise them.

The **centre** is the middle point of the circle.

The **diameter** is the widest distance across the circle, through the centre. It is twice the radius.

diameter = 2 × radius
radius = diameter ÷ 2

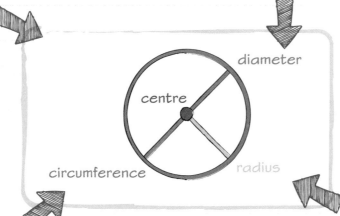

The **circumference** is the distance all the way around the edge of the circle (the perimeter).

The **radius** is distance from the edge of the circle to the centre.

The radius is half the length of the diameter, so the radius is half of 8 cm.

Example

What is the radius of a circle that has a diameter of 8 cm?

8 cm ÷ 2 = 4 cm

Now try this

1. Write the name of the feature that the red line shows for each circle.

a)

b)

c)

Coordinates

When you understand **coordinates**, you can identify and plot points on a grid.

Reading coordinates

The first number inside the brackets is the x-coordinate. This tells you how many to go right or left from the origin. The second number inside the bracket is the y-coordinate. This tells you how many to go up or down.

Plotting coordinates

The **origin** is the point where the axes meet or cross.

The coordinate grid can be divided into four sections called **quadrants**.

negative x-coordinates and positive y-coordinates

positive x-coordinates and y-coordinates

negative x-coordinates and y-coordinates

positive x-coordinates and negative y-coordinates

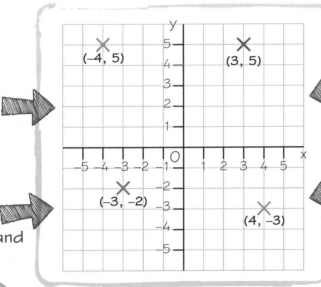

Example

Write down the coordinates of the vertices of this parallelogram.

(2, 3) (−1, 3) (−2, −2) (1, −2)

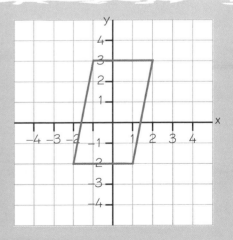

Now try this

1. Plot these points on a grid, and find the coordinates of the fourth vertex of the square.   (0, 3)   (−2, 1)   (0, −1)

Translations

Translation in maths means moving an object. You need to be able to translate simple shapes on a grid and give the coordinates of its new position.

Here are some different translations of the **red shape**.

> When a shape is translated it is not changed in any way.

B is five squares to the left.

C is three squares up.

A is two squares to the right.

D is four squares down.

E is three squares left and five squares down.

two squares to the right

$(1, 0) \rightarrow (3, 0)$ $(3, 1) \rightarrow (5, 1)$

Add 2 to the x-coordinate of each vertex.

four squares down

$(1, 0) \rightarrow (1, -4)$ $(3, 1) \rightarrow (3, -3)$

Subtract 4 from the y-coordinate of each vertex.

> When translating shapes, move each vertex the correct number of squares right, left, up, down or diagonally.

Example

> Subtract 3 from the x-coordinates and add 5 to the y-coordinates.

A triangle has coordinates $(1, -4)$, $(1, -1)$ and $(2, -1)$.
Give the coordinates of the vertices of this triangle after it has been translated **three squares to the left** and **five squares up**.

$(1, -4)$ becomes $(-2, 1)$ $(1, -1)$ becomes $(-2, 4)$ $(2, -1)$ becomes $(-1, 4)$

Now try this

1. Give the coordinates of the triangle in the example if it is translated:
   a) four squares to the left   b) two squares down

Reflection

You need to be able to **reflect** simple shapes in the x-axis or y-axis and give the coordinates of the shape in its new position.

Reflecting in the y-axis

Only the x-coordinate changes. The y-coordinate stays the same.

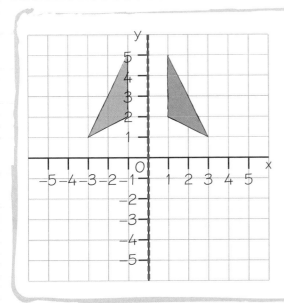

When the blue triangle is reflected in the y-axis, it becomes the green triangle.

$(1, 2) \rightarrow (-1, 2)$ $(3, 1) \rightarrow (-3, 1)$
$(1, 5) \rightarrow (-1, 5)$

The x-coordinate changes either from positive to negative or from negative to positive.
If it is zero, it doesn't change.

Reflecting in the x-axis

Only the y-coordinate changes. The x-coordinate stays the same.

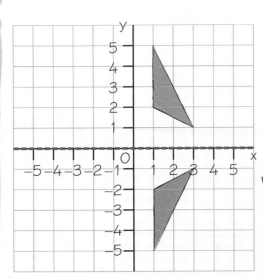

When the blue triangle is reflected in the x-axis, it becomes the purple triangle.

$(1, 2) \rightarrow (1, -2)$ $(3, 1) \rightarrow (3, -1)$
$(1, 5) \rightarrow (1, -5)$

The y-coordinate changes either from positive to negative or from negative to positive.
If it is zero, it doesn't change.

Now try this

1. The vertices of a rectangle are at (1, 1), (3, 0), (4, 2), and (2, 3).
Write down the coordinates after a reflection in:
a) the y-axis   **b)** the x-axis.

Tables

Make sure you can read from and complete tally charts, frequency tables and timetables.

Tallies and frequency tables

A **frequency table** shows how often something happens or how many things you have.

> Count the tally marks to give the frequency for each row.

This table shows the results of a survey to see how children get to school.

transport method	tally	frequency
bus	⊬⊬⊬ ‖	7
walk	‖‖	3
cycle	⊬⊬⊬ ⊬⊬⊬ ‖‖	13
car	⊬⊬⊬ ⊬⊬⊬ ⊬⊬⊬ ⊬⊬⊬ ‖‖	23

Timetables

A **timetable** shows information about the times when things happen.

Example

> Read down the first column to find the right stops. Then read across to find the departure times.

> For more on time and the 24-hour clock, see page 53.

Here is a bus timetable. It shows what time a bus leaves each stop.

Town centre	09:30	10:40	11:50	13:00	14:10	15:20
York Road	09:43	10:53	12:03	13:13	14:23	15:33
Baker Street	09:51	11:01	12:11	13:21	14:31	15:41
Library	10:07	11:17	12:27	13:37	14:47	15:57

James needs to be at the library before 2 o'clock in the afternoon. What time does the latest bus he can catch leave York Road?

> James must be on the bus that arrives at the library at 13:37

James must get on the bus at York Road at 13:13

Now try this

1. Use the timetable above. Clare gets to the bus stop in the town centre at midday. What is the earliest she can get to Baker Street?

Bar charts

Bar charts are often used to show data that is given in a table or tally chart. You should be able to use them to solve problems.

Reading a bar chart

The favourite colours of children in a class have been counted, and the data has been put into a bar chart.

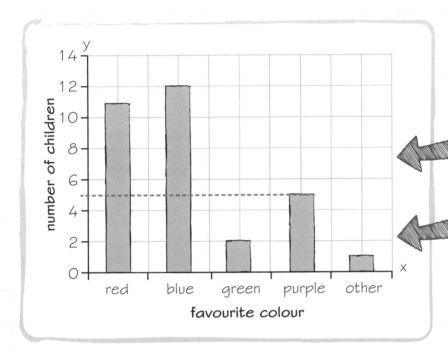

Find a colour on the bottom axis. Read across from the top of the bar to the y-axis to find how many children chose it.

5 children chose purple as their favourite colour.

Compare the height of the blue bar with the height of the green bar. What is the difference between the heights?

Example

How many more children in the class chose blue than green as their favourite colour?

12 children chose blue.
2 children chose green.
12 − 2 = 10
10 more children chose blue than green.

Now try this

Use the chart above.

1. How many children were asked in total?
2. Which colour was chosen by eleven children as their favourite?

71

Pie charts

You need to be able to read and draw **pie charts**.

Reading a pie chart

First, make sure you know what amount the whole circle stands for.
Then estimate what fraction of the whole pie each slice is.
Use this to find how many people or items each slice represents.

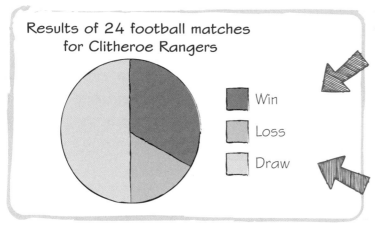

Results of 24 football matches
for Clitheroe Rangers

■ Win
■ Loss
■ Draw

The slice for wins is $\frac{1}{3}$ of the whole. $\frac{1}{3}$ of 24 matches is 8 matches.

The slice for draws is $\frac{1}{2}$ of the whole. $\frac{1}{2}$ of 24 matches is 12 matches.

> The key will tell you which category each slice of the pie chart represents.

Example

This pie chart shows the favourite fruits of 32 children.

How many more children chose strawberries than chose mangoes?

Mangoes = $\frac{1}{4}$

$\frac{1}{4}$ × 32 children = 8 children

Strawberries = $\frac{1}{2}$

$\frac{1}{2}$ × 32 children = 16 children

8 more children chose strawberries than mangoes.

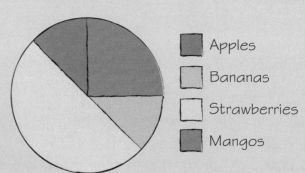

Favourite fruits

■ Apples
☐ Bananas
☐ Strawberries
■ Mangos

Now try this

Use the pie chart above.

1. How many children like apples the best?

Line graphs

Line graphs are another way of representing data. Make sure you can read them.

Reading a line graph

Line graphs are often used to show how a measurement changes over time. Time is shown along the horizontal axis.

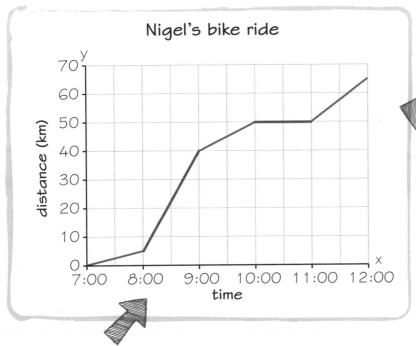

Nigel's bike ride

The flat part of the graph is when Nigel has stopped.

The distance doesn't increase.

You can either read across from the y-axis to the line and then down to the x-axis, or read up from the x-axis to the line and then across to the y-axis.

The steepest part of the graph is where Nigel rides fastest as he cycles the furthest distance in this hour.

Example

How far had Nigel cycled by 11 am?

50 km

Read up from 11:00 to the line and across to see how many kilometres he had travelled.

Now try this

Use the graph above.

1. At what time did Nigel start cycling?
2. How far had Nigel cycled by midday?
3. At what time did he reach:　　**a)** 40 km　　**b)** 50 km?

Drawing line graphs

You need to be able to plot points and complete line graphs from given data.

Plotting points

For each point, go across from the vertical scale and up from the horizontal scale and mark where the two meet.

Once all the points on the graph have been plotted, join each of the adjacent points with a straight line using a ruler.

Example

Kim goes on a bike ride and records how far she travels in a table.

Draw a line graph of the data in the table.

time	7:00	8:00	9:00	10:00	11:00	12:00
distance (km)	0	10	25	35	55	65

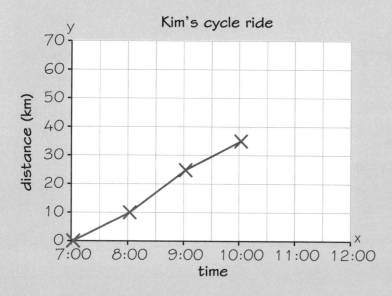

Kim's cycle ride

Time is on the x-axis, so count across to find the time. Distance is on the y-axis so count up to find the distance.

Now try this

1. Work out where the last two points should be plotted on the graph. Join the points with straight lines.

2. Tim and Yasmin hold a book sale to raise money for charity. They use a table to record how many books they have sold through the day.
   Draw a line graph of the data in the table.

time	9:00	10:00	11:00	12:00	13:00	14:00
number of books sold	4	8	16	18	24	28

Mean average

The average of a set of numbers is the typical value. The **mean** is a type of average that you need to understand and be able to calculate.

Finding the mean

To find the mean, add together all of the values, and then divide your answer by the number of values.

> Six children have the following numbers of marbles each:
> 4, 1, 10, 6, 4 and 5
>
> Total number of marbles = 4 + 1 + 10 + 6 + 4 + 5
> = 30
>
> Number of children = 6
>
> Mean = 30 ÷ 6
> = 5

If all the marbles were shared out equally among the children, each child would have 5 marbles, so the mean is 5

Example

Find the mean of each of these sets of values.

a) 5, 7, 4, 4, 3, 2, 6, 1   **b)** 7, 8, 5, 7, 4, 4, 3, 2, 6, 1

a) 5 + 7 + 4 + 4 + 3 + 2 + 6 + 1 = 32
   32 ÷ 8 values = 4   so the mean is 4

b) 7 + 8 + 5 + 7 + 4 + 4 + 3 + 2 + 6 + 1 = 47
   47 ÷ 10 values = 4.7   so the mean is 4.7

> Find the total. Divide by the number of values.

Now try this

> The mean can be a decimal number.

1. Find the mean of these five lengths: 5 cm, 7 cm, 11 cm, 9 cm, 8 cm.

2. Clive runs these distances in the days of one week: 7 km, 8 km, 12 km, 9 km, 11 km, 6 km, 3 km. What is the mean distance he runs each day?

Mean problems

You can find a missing value when you already know the mean.

Finding a missing value

Six children each have some marbles, but one child's marbles are hidden. Here are the numbers of marbles each child has: 4, 1, ?, 10, 5, 6

The mean number of marbles each child has is 5

Total number of marbles	$= 5 \times 6$
	$= 30$
Number of marbles known	$= 4 + 1 + 10 + 5 + 6$
	$= 26$
Hidden number of marbles	$= 30 - 26$
	$= 4$

There are 4 hidden marbles.

First work out the total.

This is the mean multiplied by the number of values.

Then use subtraction to find what the missing value must be.

Example

The mean of the numbers on these cards is 8. One card has been placed face-down. What number is on the card?

Total = mean × number of values
      = 8 × 5
      = 40
The total is 40 so 6 + 9 + 9 + 7 + ? = 40
The missing value must be 9

There are 5 values, so multiplying the mean by 5 will give you the total.

Now try this

1. Find the missing number if the mean of these ten numbers is six:
   8, 4, 7, 9, 6, 10, 2, 6, 2, ?

2. Find the missing number if the mean of the seven numbers is ten:
   12, 13, 9, 7, 11, 10, ?

Answers

NUMBER

1 Place value

1. *a)* 60   **b)** 10,000   **c)** 800,000

2. 420,612

3. *a)* Twelve thousand, eight hundred and fifty

    b) Five hundred and seventy-six thousand, two hundred

    c) Eight million, seven hundred thousand, four hundred and fifty

2 Negative numbers

1. −9   **2.** 17   **3.** −4 °C

3 Decimal numbers

1. 0.14   0.399   0.4   0.414   0.44   4.4

2. Example answer: 2.34   3.24   3.42   4.23

3. £5.10

4 Rounding

1. 5,800

2. 9,000,000

3. 21,250

5 Rounding decimals

1. 6.3

2. 5.57

6 Roman numerals

1. *a)* Five past nine or 9:05   **b)** Twenty to eleven or 10:40

2. *a)* 2020   **b)** 1066   *c)* 1970

7 Number and rounding problems

1. Example answers: 2.234 and 2.766 or 1.008 and 3.992

2. 150

CALCULATION

8 Written addition

1. 9,974   **2.** 83,165   **3.** 101,490

9 Written subtraction

1. 908   **2.** £31,913   **3.** 2,477 miles

10 Estimating

1. *a)* 17,000   **b)** £21   **c)** 8

2. £15

11 Add/subtract problems

1. 5,250

2. 1.15 metres

12 Multiples

1. 64   72

2. Example answer: Yes, because 12,000 × 3 = 36,000 and 6 × 6,000 = 36,000

3. Yes, because 20 × 12 = 240

13 Factors

1. 32   16

2. *a)* false: 21 is a multiple of 7

   b) false: 7 is a factor of 21

   c) true

   d) false

14 Prime numbers

1. 53   59

2. Yes, because all prime numbers except 2 are odd and if you add two odd numbers together you will always get an even number.

3. Yes, because any number that ends in 5 is divisible by 5

15 Square numbers

1. *a)* 49   *b)* 81   *c)* 100

2. 250,000 plants

16 Cube numbers

1. *a)* 343   *b)* 729   *c)* 1,000

2. 64 cups

17 Short multiplication

1. 5,222   2. £147.24   3. 12,586 passengers

18 Long multiplication

1. 317,888

2. £164,866

19 Short division

1. 1,696   2. £370   3. 52 pages

20 Long division

1. 108 r16 or $108\frac{1}{4}$ or 108.25

2. £120.50

3. 12 pencils

21 Order of operations

1. 14

2. 88

22 Solving problems

1. 63 miles

2. A drink costs £2.55 and a hot dog costs £3.75

23 Answering the question

1. 85 whole packs

2. $6\frac{1}{2}$ or 6.5

FRACTIONS, DECIMALS AND PERCENTAGES

24 Fractions

1. $\frac{6}{18} = \frac{1}{3}$

2. $\frac{12}{18} = \frac{2}{3}$

25 Equivalent fractions

1. $\frac{8}{20}$ and $\frac{5}{20}$

2. $\frac{1}{3}$

26 Fractions greater than 1

1. $\frac{7}{2}$

2. $8\frac{1}{4}$

27 Comparing fractions

1. $\frac{1}{3} < \frac{3}{7} < \frac{4}{6}$

2. Ben $\left(\frac{7}{9}\right)$ has completed more than Ella $\left(\frac{6}{9}\right)$.

28 Adding and subtracting fractions

1. $4\frac{1}{8}$　　2. $3\frac{1}{9}$　　3. $\frac{1}{8}$ of the children come to school by car.

29 Multiplying fractions

1. $\frac{1}{10}$　　2. $\frac{3}{16}$　　3. $\frac{2}{3}$

30 Dividing fractions

1. $\frac{1}{8}$　　　　2. $\frac{1}{15}$　　　　3. $\frac{1}{8}$ (3 sweets)

31 Equivalent fractions and decimals

1. 0.8　　　　2. 0.5　　　　3. 0.375

32 Multiplying decimals

1. 15

2. 15.75

33 Percentages

1. 50%

2. 25%

34 Converting percentages

1. 0.65

2. 74%

3. 0.15

35 Percentages of amounts

1. 800　　　　2. 157.5　　　　3. 352 apples are green.

36 Solving percentage problems

1. 20% of 900 = 180 but 80% of 250 = 200, so 80% of 250 is greater.

2. Alex got 35 right but James got 40, so James got more correct answers.

3. Casey saved £9 but Amerjeet saved £12, so Amerjeet saved the most.

RATIO AND PROPORTION

37 Ratio

1. $18 : 12 = 3 : 2$ 2. $4 : 3$

38 Proportion

1. $\frac{7}{10}$ 2. $\frac{1}{2}$ 3. $\frac{6}{36} = \frac{1}{6}$

39 Scale factors

1. 20 cm
2. A scale factor of $\frac{1}{10}$ was used.
3. 20 cm

40 Unequal sharing and grouping

1. 30 sweets
2. Jack received £10; Thomas received £30

41 Ratio problems

1. 5 kg would cost £10 and you could buy 750 g with £1.50
2. 12 boys and 20 girls

ALGEBRA

42 Using letters

1. $n + 7 = 20, n = 13$
2. a) $b = 6$ b) $m = 5$ c) $p = 20$

43 Simple formulae

1. £38.50
2. £72.50

44 Linear sequences

1. 29, 26, 23; term-to-term rule is 'first term = 50, subtract 3'.
2. 17, 14, 11, 8, 5, 2, −1, −4

45 Two unknowns

1. a) false
   b) true
   c) true
2. When $n = 6, m = 5$
   When $n = 5, m = 4$
   When $n = 4, m = 3$
   When $n = 3, m = 2$
   When $n = 2, m = 1$
3. When $a = 1, b = 5$
   When $a = 2, b = 6$

46 Combination problems

1.

strawberry with milk	strawberry with ice cream
kiwi with milk	kiwi with ice cream
banana with milk	banana with ice cream
mango with milk	mango with ice cream

47 Algebra problems

1. $a = 20, b = 5$

MEASUREMENT

48 Reading scales

1. *a)* 0.8 kg or 800 g
   b) 66 mph
   c) 640 g
   d) 900 ml

49 Converting units

1. *a)* 5.8 cm
   b) 150 cm
   c) 7.04 kg
2. 4,250 g
3. 3,575 ml

50 Ordering measures

1. 482 ml, $\frac{1}{2}$ l, 742 ml, $\frac{3}{4}$ ml, $\frac{4}{5}$ l, 820 ml
2. 200 g, $\frac{1}{4}$ kg, $\frac{3}{4}$ kg, 2 kg, 2,500 g, 3 kg

51 Imperial units

1. *a)* 320 km
   b) 25 miles
2. 1250 ml

52 Measure calculations

1. 2.682 litres
2. 8.4 m
3. 21.1 km

53 Time

1. 18:45
2. 20:10

54 Perimeter and area

1. D (24 cm)
2. B (36 cm²)

55 Compound shapes

1. 30 cm

56 Areas of triangles

1. *a)* 6 cm²
   b) 12 cm²

57 Areas of parallelograms

1. *a)* Area: 21 cm²   Perimeter: 22 cm
   b) Area: 30 cm²   Perimeter: 24 cm

58 Volumes of cuboids

1. 24 cm³
2. It is 8 times as large.

GEOMETRY

59 2D shape properties

1. a) irregular (isosceles) triangle

   b) irregular rhombus

   c) irregular hexagon

   d) regular octagon

60 Naming 2D shapes

1. a) scalene triangle

   b) heptagon

   c) rhombus

   d) trapezium

61 Naming 3D shapes

1. a) cube: 6 faces, 8 vertices, 12 edges

   b) square-based pyramid: 5 faces, 5 vertices, 8 edges

   c) hexagonal prism: 8 faces, 12 vertices, 18 edges

   d) pentagonal-based pyramid: 6 faces, 6 vertices, 10 edges

62 Nets

1. a) triangular prism
   b) square-based pyramid
   c) tetrahedron

63 Angles

1. 47°, acute

64 Calculating angles

1. 22°

65 Drawing 2D shapes

1. An accurate drawing of a right-angled triangle with a 7 cm base and one angle of 35°

2. An accurate drawing of an isosceles triangle with an 8 cm base and two angles of 73°

66 Circles

1. a) radius
   b) circumference
   c) diameter

67 Coordinates

1. (2, 1)

68 Translations

1. a) (1, −4) becomes (−3, −4), (1, −1) becomes (−3, −1), (2, −1) becomes (−2, −1)

   b) (1, −4) becomes (−1, −2), (1, −1) becomes (1, −3), (2, −1) becomes (2, −3)

69 Reflection

1. a) (−1, 1), (−3, 0), (−4, 2), (−2, 3)

   b) (1, −1), (3, 0), (4, −2), (2, −3)

STATISTICS

70 Tables

1. 13:21

71 Bar charts

1. 31
2. red

72 Pie charts

1. 4

73 Line graphs

1. 7:00
2. 65 km
3. a) 9:00
   b) 10:00

74 Drawing line graphs

1. (11:00, 55) and (12:00, 65)

2.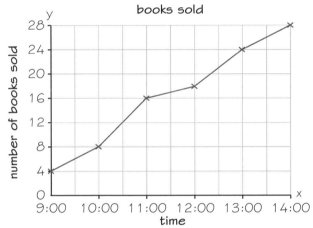

75 Mean average

1. 8 cm
2. 8 km

76 Mean problems

1. 6
2. 8

Published by Pearson Education Limited, 80 Strand, London, WC2R 0RL.

www.pearsonschools.co.uk

Text © Pearson Education Limited 2016
Edited by Saskia Besier
Typeset by Jouve India Private Limited
Produced by Elektra Media
Original illustrations © Pearson Education Limited 2016
Illustrated by Elektra Media
Cover illustration by Ana Albero

The rights of Paul Flack, Hilary Koll and Steve Mills to be identified as authors of this work has been asserted by them in accordance with the Copyright, Designs and Patents Act 1988.

First published 2016

19 18 17 16
10 9 8 7 6 5 4 3 2 1

British Library Cataloguing in Publication Data
A catalogue record for this book is available from the British Library.

ISBN 978 1 292 14626 3

Printed in Slovakia by Neografia